James McCosh

Philosophy of Reality

Should it be favored by America?

James McCosh

Philosophy of Reality
Should it be favored by America?

ISBN/EAN: 9783337077464

Printed in Europe, USA, Canada, Australia, Japan

Cover: Foto ©ninafisch / pixelio.de

More available books at **www.hansebooks.com**

PHILOSOPHY OF REALITY

PHILOSOPHY OF REALITY

SHOULD IT BE FAVORED BY AMERICA?

BY

JAMES McCOSH, LL. D., D. D., Lit. D.
EX-PRESIDENT OF PRINCETON COLLEGE

NEW YORK
CHARLES SCRIBNER'S SONS
1894

The Riverside Press, Cambridge, Mass., U. S. A.
Electrotyped and Printed by H. O. Houghton and Company.

PREFACE.

THIS little work embraces the article I read at the great exhibition at Chicago on " Reality : What Place it should hold in Philosophy." It also contains my little work, " The Prevailing Types of Philosophy: Can they logically reach Reality?"

The work is, to some extent, negative and undermining; it points out a chasm in modern philosophy. I would not give it to the public were it not that I have previously presented the positive and constructive side in my larger work on " First and Fundamental Truth." I wish the two works to go together, as constituting what I have been able to do for fundamental philosophy.

Agnosticism is upheld and propagated in the present day by several influential men, such as Mr. Herbert Spencer and Professor Huxley. It is in the air, and our young men have to breathe it and suffer the consequences. It is evidently exercising a relaxing influence on the faith and doctrinal convictions of the rising generation. It is in my view the grand office, at present, of the higher philosophy, to meet and expose this doubting spirit.

The question is, are the philosophies of the day fitted to do this?

With our eyes open, we are apt to look on the scene at some distance, rather than on things that are pressingly near and supposed to be known. So it is with modern metaphysicians (it was different with the ancient Greeks);[1] they direct their attention to more remote objects rather than those which are close to us, such as Reality.

We know self and certain things around us as Real; as having τὸ ὄν, Ens, Being, Existence. Now this Reality requires to be carefully considered by students of the First Philosophy, as Aristotle happily called it. I am to show that Reality is a truth to be assumed, and that no attempt need or should be made to establish it by mediate proof. Of those who have made the attempt, it will be found that they have more in the conclusion than they have in the premises, and that in fact they have assumed reality in order to prove it.

Mr. Spencer, the most comprehensive speculator of the day, has brought philosophy to a crisis. He is doing for later speculation, especially that of Kant and Hamilton, what Hume did for the systems of Descartes, Locke, and Berkeley, that is, bringing them to a *reductio ad absurdum* by showing that they deprive us of all knowledge of the nature of things. Philosophy has to start anew on the track of realism. I am not satisfied with the agnostic position of Spencer; I am also dissatisfied with the replies commonly made to him;[2] they have tried to prove reality, instead of showing that we are entitled to assume it.

[1] See *Appendix A.*   [2] See *infra*, p. 47.

I am aware that the realistic views presented in this work are so different from the prevailing ones — are, in fact, so revolutionary — that it will be needful to press them upon the attention of thinkers before they are adopted. This will have to be done by men who have greater influence among metaphysicians than I have been able to attain. Of the ultimate reception of these views on Reality (it may be somewhat modified) I have not a remaining doubt.

I acknowledge my obligations to my pupils, Professor Ormond of Princeton College, and Professor Armstrong of the Wesleyan University, Connecticut, for suggestions offered in the construction of this work; as also to another pupil, Professor Winans, Professor of Greek, Princeton, for aiding me in the collection of passages exhibiting Aristotle's doctrine of knowledge which I have stated in the Appendix.

January 1, 1894.

CONTENTS.

SECTION I.

PAGE

REALITY: WHAT PLACE IT SHOULD HOLD IN PHILOSOPHY . . . 1

SECTION II.
WAY IN WHICH REALITY IS DISCOVERED 7

SECTION III
WHAT IS REALITY? 9

SECTION IV.
GREEK PHILOSOPHY 19

SECTION V.
DESCARTES 21

SECTION VI.
THE EXPERIMENTAL SCHOOL 22

SECTION VII
THE A-PRIORI OR KANTIAN SCHOOL 24

SECTION VIII.
THE SCOTTISH SCHOOL 43

SECTION IX.
THE SENSATIONAL SCHOOL 50

x   CONTENTS.

SECTION X.

HUXLEY AND HERBERT SPENCER 55

SECTION XI.

REALISM AND RELIGION 57

SECTION XII.

THE RESULTS REACHED 58

APPENDIX.

A. ARISTOTLE ON THE COGNITIVE POWERS OF THE MIND . . . 70
B. DOCTRINE OF DR. THOMAS AQUINAS 75
C. RECENT CRITICISMS OF KANT 75
D. PLACE OF INDUCTION IN METAPHYSICS 78

PHILOSOPHY OF REALITY.

SHOULD IT BE FAVORED BY AMERICA?

SECTION FIRST.

REALITY : WHAT PLACE IT SHOULD HOLD IN PHILOSOPHY.

THIS is an important question; I regard it as the most important in philosophy in the present day. Scanty systems have arisen from the oversight of it.

I.

In establishing my positions I remark that every one believes in realities. Every one believes in two kinds of realities. He believes in his own existence. He believes or rather knows that he thinks and feels; that he is liable to grief and joy, to hope and fear. He believes and knows things without him; in that man or woman, in the various organs of his body, in that wall or house, as also in that tree before him, in the greenness of its foliage, in the hardness of its trunk, and in the smell and taste of its fruit.

We can appeal to the proper tests in justifying reality. First the objects are self-evident. We know ourselves by simply looking within, and objects around, by simply looking without. We need no further evidence. But secondly, this is confirmed by the circumstance that this belief or knowledge is necessary; we cannot be made to believe or know otherwise. We cannot be made to believe, by any argument or by any reasoning, that these objects do not exist. But all the while we have a belief or conviction which abides with us. Then, thirdly, this belief or knowledge is universal. Not only do I believe in these objects, but every man does the same. He is sure that he himself exists, and that certain objects around him exist. He carries this conviction with him wherever he goes. Philosophy, which is an expression of our nature, should do the same.

II.

Reality cannot be established by syllogistic or mediate proof of any kind. No man can prove mediately his own existence, or the pains he feels in his own body, or the existence of that stone or plant which he sees and touches. If he is not satisfied with this statement on its being announced let him try the proof. He will find that he has no mediate proof, and that he is assuming when he imagines that he is proving. To prove that there is life or mind, we must have life or mind in the premise. Without this the alleged proof will evidently be illogical. For it is acknowledged on all hands that in order to a right conclusion we must have the object or truth in the conclusion involved in the premise or premises.

The attempt to prove Reality has ever led to unmeasurable confusion and error. Descartes, the father of modern philosophy, propounded an argument, *Cogito, ergo sum.* But if the *ego* be in the *cogito*, the whole alleged argument for Reality is an evident assumption, for already we have the Reality there. If the ego be not in the *cogito*, we have no proof whatever, as what we have in the conclusion is not in the premise.

III.

Reality is got not by reasoning, but by immediate inspection, by what is usually called Intuition. We have Cognitive faculties for this purpose, especially the inward and outward senses. We know ourselves, and especially our various ideas, moods, sufferings, by self-consciousness. We know these extended things, by the senses as cognitive, particularly by sight and touch. We need no mediate proof. In regard to these things, proffered probation would be felt as an incumbrance and would turn out to be invalid.

We have here primary truth which does not need support, but which may give support to other truth reared upon it. Knowing objects to be real, we may draw other objects from them which are also real by argument, say by mathematics, by ordinary science, by common observation.

There may be times when we are not sure whether the object is a reality or a phantom, whether that whiteness seen in the darkness is a ghost or a sheet put out to be dried. We are to settle the question by an examination of the appearance, using, if need be, all the senses.

It is to be understood that when we have the real we can also have things, derived from it logically, also real. Thus having the individual oak as real, we have oaks in general as also real. The reality in the singular goes up into the general.

There are some who maintain that Realism must not only establish the reality of objects, but must show what the reality consists in. Now, I am willing to admit in establishing reality we must know somewhat of the nature of the reality. It is thus that we can separate it from other things, only thus we can think or speak of it.   Still it is not by psychological but by the physical sciences that we must determine the real nature of the object.   Mental science must know somewhat of the nature of water before it can declare it to be a reality. But it is not psychology but chemistry that must settle what this reality is, that water is composed of oxygen and hydrogen.   It is astronomy and not philosophy that must show us what is the relation of the planets one to another.

It is to be understood that while the mind has the Real by the cognitive powers, it may also have the Ideal by the imagination, and the two not inconsistent one with the other.   It may form a figure of ugliness or beauty to which there is no corresponding fact.   With these we may be amused, or we may be exalted above ourselves and above the earth.   These fancies will present themselves spontaneously, or we call them up by an act of will.   If reality has its solid blessings so has ideality its pleasing fancies.   We should profitably retain and cherish both.   But we should always distinguish between them.

I should like to inquire here how the various systems of philosophy, ancient and modern, accord with these views.   I must content myself here with reviewing one system, but that by far the most influential for the last few ages.

The prevalent philosophy in the present day is that of Kant; and this in all countries, European and American, in which philosophy is valued.   I wish it to be understood that I look on Kant as one of our great thinkers. There never can come a time when certain truths of Kant and the German philosophy are to be regarded as superseded.   But Kant was guilty of one great oversight.   He did not start with Reality in his primitive assumptions. While we cannot dispense with him, the crisis has come in which the Critical Philosophy should be critically examined, when it will turn out that its supremacy should be set aside.

Kantians of all descriptions are forever referring to space and time as forms of sense. I do not say that too much importance has been attached to space and time while light has been thrown upon them by these discussions. But along with these forms there should have been assumed Reality in the things made known to us. Reality is not an end to be gained after a process or by a process, but is a means to an end. We are to begin with Reality and carry it with us, and it should run on throughout the whole of life.

There is admirable system in the Categories and in the Ideas with which Kant follows up his Forms of Sense ; and in them Reality is not to be regarded as superseded or set aside. But if we have not Reality throughout the foundation is insecure ; and hence the vacillations through which the German philosophy has passed, and which are not to be arrested till Reality has its place to stay the whole.

Kant began with *phenomena*. But the phrase has two senses. In ordinary science it means a fact to be explained, that is referred to its law. Or it may retain its Greek meaning and signify appearance to be explained. It is in this sense that Kant uses the phrase. With these appearances he starts, and from these he never could derive and infer any real object without having in the conclusion what was not in the premises. He should have begun with Realities as made known by the consciousness and the senses. Only thus can we have a true philosophy with a well laid superstructure. A philosophy which does not thus begin with Reality must always have something insecure in its foundation.

We have come to a crisis in philosophy. We must start anew, taking with us what we have omitted, and thus rectify the oversight of which we have been guilty. No philosophy is to be accepted which does not hold resolutely by Reality.

It is well known that German philosophy has been largely swaying German theology. It is worthy of inquiry whether the neglect of Reality has not been injuring both its philosophy and its theology, and has been injuriously affecting both the philosophy and theology of Great Britain and America, and been the sources of their vacillation in late years. Even the first truth in theology implies Reality, "for the invisible things of God are clearly seen from the things that are made," which *things that are made* clearly imply Reality.

Hitherto America has had no special philosophy as the ancient Greeks had, as the Scotch have had, and the Germans have had. But there is a philosophy lying before it, and it should appropriate it, and call it its own — an advance beyond Locke, beyond the Scottish School — the American philosophy. This would be in thorough accordance with the American character which claims to be so practical.

The change from the speculative to this thoroughly realistic philosophy would not be unlike that from the European Monarchies to the American Republics. Where could this be inaugurated so appropriately and auspiciously as at the World's Great Exposition?

SECTION SECOND.

WAY IN WHICH REALITY IS DISCOVERED.

STARTING in this way with real objects, we prosecute farther investigations by Induction. This is the method pursued by Reid and the Scottish School. It was derived originally from Francis Bacon, and had already reached many important results in physics in the discoveries of Sir Isaac Newton and others. The Scottish School perceived this, and were anxious to secure like results by the same method in the study of the human mind, using self-consciousness rather than the senses in the gathering of the facts. In this way they had been so far successful as may be seen in the account which Reid, Stewart, and others had given of the faculties of the mind. Not that they for one instant regarded this Induction as the foundation of their philosophy, which had its foundation within itself in the principles of common sense and the fundamental laws of thought and belief. But they represented Induction as the means of discovering these laws. Thus they built up a philosophy resting on deeper principles, but discovered by the cautious and safe method of Induction.

We may consider more carefully the way in which reality is discovered. Take this stone and this tree: I perceive them to be realities at once by the sense of sight and the sense of touch, and I cannot be made to decide otherwise. I cannot prove it immediately or by syllogism, for I have no prior premises to establish the point that this stone exists, that this tree exists. It is the same with any other object, such as this chair and this table, this door and this window, this church or this steeple. The mind has cognitive powers by which it discerns these objects, that they exist.

By the same or further cognitive powers it may come to know further qualities of these objects ; of this stone that it is hard, or of that log that it is brittle ; or of this tree that it grows slowly or grows rapidly ; of this chair that it can hold only one person ; of this table that it is square ; of this door that it is wide; of this window that it is narrow ; of this church that it can hold a thousand people ; of this steeple that it is one hundred feet high. Thus we may increase our knowledge of objects from day to day till the number comes beyond our calculation.

When there is an addition or multiplication of real objects, there is no lessening or increasing of this reality, which continues the same. In the same way, by the inner sense or reflection, we at once discover, not by reasoning, something in our hope and grief and joy. Having reality in the individual stone or tree, we have reality in the general notion in stones or trees. Having reality in the qualities of the concrete object, we have reality in the abstract; thus, reality in the stone implies reality in its qualities of hardness.

Reality is in all these quarters. I think we are entitled to call the inquiry into, and the results which issue from it, the Philosophy of Realism, and to adopt it as the true philosophy.

SECTION THIRD.

I.

EVERYBODY knows the existence of Reality; or, to vary the phrase when we speak of things acting, every one knows Actuality.

Of all thoughts, or perhaps I should rather say of all perceptions, it seems to be the clearest. Yet it is one of the most difficult to explain, or even express. This is simply because it is so simple: it does not admit of analysis; it has no distinct elements into which to resolve it, and there is no common genus or species under which to place it. The only way of showing its nature is to point to examples of it. We look on the wall of the room in which we sit, and know it to be real. We see a bird flying, and know it to be an actuality. We are conscious of ourselves in pain, and we are sure of our own existence in a state of pain.

There may be realities which we cannot discover: we do not know whether the planet Jupiter is inhabited. But there are things which we know to be real. We know body as it is presented to us as extended and exercising power or properties. In self-consciousness we know self as feeling, knowing, willing. Thus we know the manifestations of body, such as shape, resistance, and mobility. Thus we know the manifestations of self, as knowledge, desire, resolution. The qualities which we perceive in ourselves, specially such as love, benevolence, justice, are actualities. All these differ from imaginations, say a fairy, a ghost, a mermaid; and commonly the two can be distinguished. We call the one real, the other unreal.

II.

We cannot explain or even understand the facts of which we are conscious without calling in two cognitive powers, the external and the internal senses. These cannot be resolved into anything else, say, as is often attempted, into sensations, impressions, ideas; for none of these contain cognition, and cannot, therefore, give us knowledge by accumulation or combination. Nor can knowledge be drawn from them by reasoning; for, not being in the premises, they cannot reach it, except by falling into the acknowledged fallacy of having more in the conclusion than in the premises.

In acquiring a knowledge of external things, sensations are involved; feelings in the organism by all the senses: but these not having knowledge cannot give it to us logically. In looking at the table before us, there is the exercise of coats and humors, of rods and cones, and of the optic nerve; but we do not notice these in vision; their existence has been made known to us by the physiologist. In hearing, the tympanum, the hammer, the stirrup, and auditory nerve do not form part of our intuitive knowledge; they are merely the means of giving an exact field to our perceptions, but are no part of the reality directly perceived by us. With these concurrences we look immediately upon the thing, as we look through perfectly transparent glass upon the tree without noticing the medium.

In standing up for realism it is to be understood that we hold by the known actuality of mind, with its perceptions, thoughts, and feelings, as well as of matter with its extension and force. We have as clear a perception of the one as of the other. We know both by a power of intuition or direct inspection; the one by perception of the senses, the other by self-consciousness. We know each of them by its peculiar properties: the one as resisting our energy and extended in three dimensions; the other, as knowing and judging with appetencies and feelings. We possess these knowing powers naturally; we carry them with us at all times; they are in our very nature and constitution.

It is to be noticed that we know not only body and mind: we know the affections or qualities of both; indeed, it is by, or rather with, their qualities that we know the substances. We know extension and solidity in matter; cognition and emotion in mind. In particular we should insist that we know moral qualities, such as good and evil, and the obligation lying upon us to do the one and avoid the other. It is of the utmost importance in ethics to claim that there is a known reality in these moral qualities, quite as much so as there is extension in body and perception in mind.

III.

But it is asked contemptuously, Do you really believe that we perceive things as they are? that things really are what they appear to us? If you say so, then you must hold that a man in a mist is larger than when in

clear air; that the sun when setting has a more expanded
surface than at midday; that the sky is not an expanse,
but a concave firmament; that the ocean as we look on
it from the shore is a perfect level, without any curva-
ture; that the lines in a railway draw nearer to each
other as they recede; that a measured mile seen across
an arm of the sea is longer than when seen across hill
and dale on land. Such puzzles seem to show that, whatever supposed things be, they are not what they appear
to us to be. Pointing to these difficulties, sceptical philosophers argue that we can never discover realities. The
great body of philosophers employ themselves in showing
how reality is to be reached by a process which they
point out. I believe that none of the theories which they
advance are satisfactory.

In order to remove the perplexities which have gath-
ered round the subject, it is of importance to clear up
two points: First, what are the realities which we profess to discover? These are: —

1. All that we know by intuition, that is, by an immediate perception of the object. Thus we know matter as
extended and resisting our energy. We also know mind
as knowing, thinking, feeling, resolving. Of this intuitive knowledge there are three criteria clear and decisive.
First, it is self-evident. We know the object at once on
looking at it. In looking at the table, I am sure there is
a colored surface before me. Being thus self-evident, it
is, Secondly, necessary; we cannot be made to believe
otherwise. Thirdly, it is universal, that is, held by all
men on the objects being presented to them. These are
the tests of primary truths, and they sanction the conviction that we know realities. 2. All that is drawn from
this by logical deduction. Ever since the time of Aristotle we have had a test of the legitimacy of inference

in the syllogism, which is expounded in the treatises of formal logic. 3. All that is got by scientific induction. We have tests of the legitimacy of this in the Prerogative Instances of Bacon, and more especially in John S. Mill's Canons of Induction, expounded in the books of Inductive Logic. To this class of realities belong the ascertained laws of nature, such as gravitation, chemical affinity, the association of ideas. In these we rise above the individual facts revealed by external and internal perception, and correlate the facts. The laws thus reached are not apodictic, or demonstrative like mathematical truths. But they are to be accepted provisionally as realities, which, it is allowed, may be modified and rectified by advancing discoveries; thus gravitation is a reality, but may possibly be resolved in the end, as its discoverer believed, into a higher reality.

IV.

Secondly, in order to determine the precise reality, we have to draw certain distinctions. I have unfolded these elsewhere,[1] but to make our discussion complete it is expedient to repeat them here, and apply them to the subject before us. Our object is to determine the reality, and we have: —

1. To distinguish between the real object and the sensations and feelings associated with it; generally between our sensations and perceptions. The former of these have indeed a sort of reality as affections of self, and they have no external reality, and we fall into error when we suppose that they have.

2. As the most important, we have to distinguish between our original and acquired perceptions. From an

[1] See *First and Fundamental Truths*, part ii. book i. ch. iii.

early period of our lives, during infancy and at all later dates, these two are closely associated with each other, and it is at times difficult to distinguish them. We claim a certainty in our original perceptions only; there may be error in our derived perceptions, and no reality in them.

I believe we can determine precisely what we know intuitively and directly by the various senses. The eye gives us a colored surface, nothing more. Hearing gives us a sound in the ear, from which we argue a cause, which is found by science to be undulations. In smell we have an affection of the nostrils; in taste, an affection of the palate; in touch proper, or feeling, an affection of the part from which the afferent nerve comes. In the muscular sense and energy, we have resistance offered, implying resisting energy. These are our primary sense-cognitions, all noticed by self-consciousness; they reveal realities, and upon them, by legitimate processes, we may rear other knowledges, also of reality, as derived from what is real. But we may also draw erroneous deductions when we pass beyond our intuitive knowledge. We do not know distance intuitively by the eye or by the ear, and we declare that the rock seen across the sea is only one mile distant, when actual measurement finds it to be two. I have shown that to preserve us from error we have to draw a like distinction in memory between our original memories and our constructed memories, in which latter there may be errors.

3. There is the distinction between the Primary and Secondary Qualities of Matter. This distinction has not always been correctly enunciated, but, when properly viewed, it has a most important place in determining what reality there is in the supposed qualities of matter. The Primary Qualities, such as extension and resisting

energy, are perceived, as Reid has remarked, directly;
and are in all matter, as Locke has shown. These always
imply realities. The Secondary Qualities are reached
by argument, and the conclusion may not be correctly
drawn. Thus in heat there is a reality in the organic
sensation; but the external cause, supposed to be a mode
of motion, is discoverable only by a scientific process, to
be tested by the canons of induction.

By calling in such obvious principles and distinctions
as these, we are able to stand up for the trustworthiness
of the senses. What we see intuitively by the eye is not
the sky, or the sea, or the rock, or the man in the mist,
at a distance, but the object on the eye which is always
real.

We are thus able without difficulty to determine what
is real within us and around us more satisfactorily than is
commonly done by metaphysicians, by a process which,
if we examine it, will be seen to reach reality only by
unknowingly assuming it.

V.

As to this knowledge, it should always be understood
that it is only partial. "We know in part." This doctrine is opposed, on the one hand, to Gnosticism, which
claims to know all; and, on the other hand, to Agnosticism, which professes to know nothing. Between these
two we should hold by Mereognosticism, which holds
that we know, but only in part. What we do know we
should stand by, or rather stand upon, as a foundation
to give us stability, and on which we may rear other realities.

As we all spontaneously believe in, or rather know,
reality, so it should have a place, a deep and a thoroughly

pervading place, in all philosophic systems. Whatever else philosophy may be, it is a science of foundations, and should commence with and rest upon the reality of things as a basis. An intellectual system which does not contain and embrace actuality must be a speculation rather than a philosophy.

We should not attempt to prove reality by mediate proof. Indeed, it cannot be demonstrated by any such process. The very constitutive principle of Logic or inference is, that there be nothing in the conclusion which was not contained in the premise (or premises). If reality be not in the premise, you cannot legitimately get it in the conclusion. The conclusion we reach here is, that in all philosophy we must assume reality. Beyond this we can do nothing more than show that we are entitled to assume it.

Not that it is to be represented as unproven and unprovable; it has its proof in itself. Not that it is to be described, as it often is in the present day, as unknown and unknowable; it is the first known, the best known of all truths. We need not try to prove it by mediate evidence, for we have immediate evidence, which is stronger, as on it mediate proof must depend in the last resort. It does not need other evidence, it has its evidence in itself; it is self-evident. It does not require external support; it stands on its own basis, and gives support to other truths. You cannot find any other truth clearer or more certain by which to establish it. Any external probation might rather unsettle it as tending to throw it off its proper foundation. We do not reach it by a process; it is rather the starting-point of many processes. It is not a conclusion reached; it is a premise necessary to innumerable conclusions.

It is possible, indeed, speculatively and in words, to

deny reality. But naturally and spontaneously we know
all the while that the very denial implies the existence
of the one who makes the denial. A man may affirm that
the river before him does not exist; but he shows that
he believes in its existence by his declining to cast himself into it. He may say there is no carriage on the road
before him; but he hastens to go out of its way when it
approaches. He may insist that there is no sword in
that man's hand; but he turns aside when it would
pierce him. He may assure us that he does not exist;
but in the very declaration he manifests his own existence.

Now, the question I have to ask is, What do the leading philosophic systems of the day make of reality? I
am to put this question to each of them. Do they acknowledge it, or do they deny it? Do they accept it in
whole, or only in part? Do they attempt to prove it, or
simply assume it ?

Some acknowledge that there is reality in certain objects and deny it in certain others, both of which are
supported by the same intuitive evidence. Thus some
claim that there is actuality revealed by the external
senses, but not by the internal sense, and are landed in
materialism. Others hold firmly by what we know of
mind or self, but discard the fleeting phenomena of bodily senses, and are idealists. Some seriously try to prove
the existence of reality; but as they evidently fail, there
are others who feel as if we have only a phenomenal
world, or a sort of dreamland. The fault of the great
body of metaphysicians has been that they have acted on
no principle, and have admitted actuality in some cases
and denied it in others, both having a like evidence or
want of evidence; and have thus made philosophy capri-
cious and inconsistent.

Let us understand definitely what is the question I put. It is not what is the belief held and acted on by the system-builders as individuals, for practically they have all acted on the reality of things. David Hume said again and again, "Though I show what are the sceptical issues of the philosophy of the day, in actual life I believe and act as other people." Nor is my question how the philosophers wished their systems to be understood. Locke and Kant both held that their systems were realistic; but both philosophies, it can be shown, were idealistic on the one hand and sceptical on the other in their logical tendencies. We may be sure that all philosophies will issue sooner or later at the place to which logic drives them.

There is a Nemesis in philosophy as there is in morality. Hume the sceptic was the Avenger who drove to its consequences the errors that prevailed from Descartes to Berkeley. Herbert Spencer is the Avenger who is leading on to Agnosticism the error that has remained in the prevailing philosophies. We shall have to inquire how we are to build on the ground which has been left waste.

Philosophy in this age takes three types: I. The SEN-SATIONAL and EXPERIENTIAL; II. The A-PRIORI or KANTIAN; III. The SCOTTISH. These stand before us as mountain chains with valleys between, but with ranges of hills proceeding from them, and at times joining on to each other. They are found not only in Great Britain and America, but in Germany, France, Italy, and all civilized countries. The question I put is, What do these make of reality?

SECTION FOURTH.

GREEK PHILOSOPHY.

HERE it may be interesting to notice that the aim of the Greek philosophy — the earliest deserving the name, all prior being loose and undiscriminating — was to discover reality as opposed to appearances. Its earliest metaphysical school was the Eleatic, and its search was for existence, — τὸ ὄν and τὸ εἶναι. In their subtle disquisitions, they often confused what is simple, and made assertions which have no meaning. It can be shown that the Greek philosophy kept it steadily in view to discover, not the absolute, as the German historians so often represent them as doing, but the real. This was the aim of Socrates when he insisted so much on definition. Plato found the real among the fleeting in his Ideas. Aristotle classified the real under his ten Categories. The Stoics found reality specially in virtue as the only good, and the Epicureans in pleasure. It was because this was their search that the Greek philosophy has been so abiding, and that students ever turn back to it, while other systems have been swallowing each other and have had only a temporary sway. So, then, as we assume spontaneously the existence of a self and a non-self, let us also assume it in philosophy, as the reflex expression of our spontaneities. Philosophy should commence with it, and take it with it by implication wherever it goes. In all its investigations, it should presuppose and proceed upon it. A philosophy without it is a speculation and not truth.[1]

The relation between mind and body has always been regarded as a mystery which we cannot thoroughly clear up. Yet we may reverently inquire what the process is, and state what it is so far as we know it. Mr. J. S. Mill has shown that all physical causation is dual or plural; it consists of two or more agents constituting the cause, and producing a change on each of the agents. A blow is inflicted on a man's brain which causes his death; here the cause is the blow and the state of the brain, and the effect, the death, is the joint result of the two. So in Sense-Perception there is an outward object, — it may be in the body or beyond the body, and thus standing in a particular relation to the mind; the effect is the perception of the object. So, in all cases, there is a mutual affection of the external object, which in the last resort is the nerves and brain on the one hand, and on the other hand the mind, with its perceptive power; and the result is a perception of the object. This seems to be a statement of the facts. There is no doubt mystery, that is, some things which we do not understand; but there is no more mystery than in any other causation: the two agents have the property of acting on each other. But if this be the true account, possibly after all only a partial account, we are delivered from all the useless intermediaries which metaphysicians of late ages have introduced to explain what they do not explain, and which may need no explanation. Aristotle briefly expresses the exact facts: "The sensible objects call the perceptive sense into activity."[2]

[1] See *Appendix A.*   [2] See *Appendix A.*

SECTION FIFTH.

DESCARTES.

THIS doctrine of Reality following the Greek philosophy continued during the middle ages, except among the small body of sceptics, but all this was changed by Descartes, the great philosopher of the French School. *Cogito ergo sum* was his aphorism, thereby seeking to strengthen his belief in reality of self, founding it upon argument, with a premise and a conclusion. But if the ego be in the cogito, the conclusion is a mere pleonasm. If the ego be not in the cogito, the conclusion does not follow, and the conclusion is not legitimate. Some have denied that this is really an argument. It is represented as a primitive judgment, seen by them to be true at once. But surely Descartes knew what an argument was ; and when he put his statement in the form of an argument, he must have regarded it as such ; but in doing this he did not properly express the process that passes in the human mind, which is not *Cogito ergo sum*, but *ego cognitans* assumed. This is a truth on which other truths may rest. But from that day to this, philosophy has always had some sort of process in the way in which we know *ourselves*.

SECTION SIXTH.

THE EXPERIENTIAL SCHOOL.

LOCKE may be regarded as a representative of this school. He is not a sensationalist, though he is often so designated. Often have I heard him spoken of in the lectures of German professors by the name of Locké, as the representative sensationalist. But Locke allots to man two inlets of ideas, sensation and reflection; and attaches the greater importance to the second. To reflection we are indebted for all our ideas of mind and its qualities, of spiritual things and of God. Besides, he gives to mind a special power of intuition which perceives at once the agreement and disagreement of ideas (not of things), and thence rises to demonstration;[1] and he affirms that ethics might be made demonstrative, though he never showed how this could be done.[2]

Locke was personally a determined realist, and believed that his philosophy was realistic; but he never reached a full and satisfactory reality. Primarily, according to his theory, we perceive ideas within ourselves; knowledge is simply the perception of the agreement or disagreement of ideas, and we get all our ideas and knowledge by experience, which is limited, and can never rise above itself, any more than water can rise above its fountain. The consequence is, that he was never able to

[1] *Essay*, b. iv. ch. i.   [2] *Essay*, b. iv. 17.

reach truth above experience, to universal and necessary truth holding true in all time and in all places. He believed most firmly in God and in infinity; but, as Hume showed, he could not by mere experience prove the existence of a God who is beyond all experience of sense and consciousness.

His greatest admirers were never able to show how he could find, on his theory of knowledge, an actuality external to the mind. He tells us: " 'T is evident the mind knows not things immediately, but only by the intervention of the ideas it has of them."[1] His whole account of human understanding proceeds on this principle. He fondly held that the ideas were resemblances and representatives of things; but he had no proof of this, and did not pretend to have any. The mind perceives ideas, but does not perceive things, and therefore cannot possibly know that the ideas which it knows are copies of the things which it can never know. We are thus shut up into an ideal world, and have no means of breaking out from this shell or prison, and can never know that there is such a thing as body beyond our idea of it.

Berkeley started from this position, and followed out Locke's theory to its legitimate consequences, maintaining that ideas are the reality, and constitute the whole of the reality which man can find. Hume interposed at this point, and drove the whole process to scepticism,— to what would now be called agnosticism. We have impressions, and ideas the reproduction of impressions, and have and can have nothing else.

[1] *Essay,* iv. 1.

SECTION SEVENTH.

THE A-PRIORI OR KANTIAN SCHOOL.

I.

LOCKE'S Philosophy was the prevailing one from the date of his "Essay on Human Understanding," in 1690, to about 1830, when there was a shaking of thought, which issued in the second French Revolution and the Reform Bill of England, and a reaction in philosophy against the prevailing empiricism among conservative minds afraid of the too rapid advances of radical and revolutionary opinions. Since that time — indeed, fifty years prior in Germany — Kant's philosophy has been the prevailing one among deeper thinkers all over the thinking world. It was set up to oppose the scepticism of Hume, which awoke Kant, as he tells us, from his dogmatic slumbers. It was also meant, following Leibnitz, to counteract the empiricism and supposed sensationalism of the "very celebrated Locke," as Kant designates him.

It embraces a vast body of profound truth firmly concatenated, and has brought out more fully than was ever done before some of the deeper powers in the human mind. It reached the highest crest of the wave at the centenary, in 1881, of Kant's great work on the "Kritik of Pure Reason." I may be mistaken, but I think I see signs of late years of its being subjected to a severe questioning on the part of those who think that some of its principles are keeping us away from reality. In one of its forms, that of its high speculative ideas, it has gone up years ago into the clouds of Hegelianism, from which sober thinkers are turning away; in another form, in which it has only appearances and unknown things, it has run aground into the clay of the Agnosticism of Herbert Spencer, whom one half of our ambitious metaphysic youths are following, and the other half are criticising. It is time that we have a thorough criticism of the critical philosophy, such as we had half a century ago of the philosophy of Locke.

For years past I have been urging general objections to the system of the great German metaphysician.[1] In this paper I am simply inquiring whether it has reached and embraced reality.

The Kritic of Pure Reason, reared as a castellated structure strong and compact, is the Ehrenbretstein of German philosophy. It is a skilfully constructed, but is an artificial and not a natural product. It will be seen as we advance that it does not begin with reality, and so cannot find it as it goes on, nor end with it logically. It keeps reality at a distance, lest it should lead into materialism, which pretends to be so real. But Realism embraces both a material and a spiritual actuality, and each should have its own place in a natural system in which there is a body provided, where the spirit may dwell and appear in living form.

II.

1. *The Method pursued, the Critical, does not reveal Reality to us.* Kant acted rightly in departing from the

---

[1] See my work, *Realistic Philosophy*, vol. ii., article on " Criticism of Critical Philosophy."

Dogmatic Method, which had been used by Descartes and so many philosophers prior to his time. That method is used in mathematics, where we have axioms to start with, which we need only clearly to define. But it is not applicable in sciences which deal with scattered facts, and which we should pursue in the Inductive Method, in mental science, with self-consciousness as the agent which makes known the facts to us.

Kant takes credit for introducing a new Method, neither the Dogmatic nor the Inductive, but the Critical. Pure Reason, he says, can criticise itself. By this Method he constructed his system, which has been the admiration on the part of profound thinkers, even of those who may not regard it as the plan of Nature or of God. I acknowledge that criticism has a function to perform: it has to examine the works constructed by man, such as literary style, theories of poetry and the drama, works of art, as paintings, statues, and buildings. But we do not venture to criticise the works of Nature and of God; our business is simply to discover what these are, and to fall in with them. No one has ever ventured to construct physical science by criticism; say chemistry, or biology, or physiology. Were such an attempt made, it would issue in a series and succession of systems jostling each other, with no means of effecting a settlement. These effects have actually followed from the application of the critical methods to mental philosophy. Since the days of Kant, there has been a succession of systems superseding each other with no principle of final appeal. Every few years there appears a fresh and independent youth, proclaiming: Kant has not followed a certain principle to its consequences; let us carry it out thoroughly. It was thus that philosophy advanced from Kant to Hegel. Another says, There is a grand principle which has been overlooked: let us introduce it and it will mediate between the systems; and thus a new system has been introduced to multiply the confusion. This was the mode of procedure in ancient physics, and the Stoics had one cosmology, and the Epicureans another. All this has been abandoned in modern science; and we have a means of settling disputes, not by criticism, but by conformity of theories to the facts of Nature. The Critical Method has carried us away from Reality, and should now be let down from its high place as chief, to occupy a subordinate position.

There is a sense in which the truths both of physics and metaphysics are to be submitted to criticism. The profound wisdom of Bacon insisted on the inductive sciences beginning with "Necessary Rejections and Exclusions," and Whewell insists on the "Decomposition of Facts." But this is merely to put irrelevant matter out of the way to enable us to study by induction the facts of our nature without and within us.

Metaphysical philosophy is the science of First and Fundamental Truths, and these are to be discovered solely by the careful observation of what passes in our minds. But let it be understood that our induction of them does not give to these truths their validity; it merely enables us to observe them. This is a distinction which I have been laboring to make students of mental philosophy see and acknowledge and proceed on.[1] Induction certainly does not give authority to Primitive or *A-Priori* truth; but it is necessary in order to our being able to discover its nature, and to use it in philosophy. The careful induction of Newton did not make, create, or invent the law of gravitation, or give to it its function; but it was necessary to make it known to us.

[1] See *Appendix D.*

Such fundamental and necessary truths as personal identity, substance, causation, moral obligation, responsibility rising to a knowledge of God, are in our very nature,
and have their authority in themselves and from God.
But it is one of our highest prerogatives that we can rise
· by internal reflection and induction to the precise knowledge of these truths, and use them in philosophy and
theology.

The Kritik of the Speculative Reason embraces three
points: I. ÆSTHETIC, or the *a-priori* elements in the
Senses; II. ANALYTIC, or the *a-priori* elements in the
Understanding; III. DIALECTIC, or the *a-priori* elements
in Reason.   I am to subject these to an examination.

III.

2. In ÆSTHETIC *he misses Reality by making our
primitive perceptions look to phenomena and not to things.*
What is meant by phenomenon?   In scientific investigation it is commonly used to denote a fact revealed in
order to be referred to a law.   But in the philosophy of
Kant it is employed, in the original Greek sense of the
word, as an appearance.   According to Kant and his
school, the mind in sense-perception and in self-consciousness begins with phenomena in the sense of appearances.
This, it can be shown, prevents it from reaching realities.

It might be argued that appearance of itself implies
reality; a phenomenon is a thing appearing.   In one of
Longfellow's poems, there is a dispute between the tree
on the river's banks and the tree reflected in the waters
as to which is the reality.   The question can be settled;
there is a reality in both, but of a different kind.   The
tree on the banks has solidity, the tree in the stream is a
reflection of light.   In all appearances presented to us,

there is a thing that appears, and what we have to ascertain is the precise actuality. It can be shown that this was the search of the Greek philosophy. In the Kantian system there is an appearance presented, but this appearance is entirely subjective; that is, in the mind. The mind in perception cannot look beyond itself, and so cannot know anything external. He argues, indeed, in the preface of the second edition of the Kritik: "The real existence of things outside of us, and independently of our consciousness of them, is an assumption without which he could not have found even a beginning for his philosophy." I am glad to find him making such an assumption; it is an assumption given us by our consciousness. But he tries to prove it by a very doubtful probation. "The simple but empirically determined consciousness of my own existence proves the existence of objects in space outside of me." I cannot see that the conclusion follows from the premise. Whether assumed or proven, it is clear that he holds by the existence of external things; but the nature of these external things cannot be known by us. Even the mind itself is not known as a thing. This is one of Kant's most pernicious errors, more so than even his denial that we know anything of the nature of matter. Nothing remains, as we shall see forthwith, but a conglomerate of forms, categories, and ideas, embracing no reality beyond themselves.

We now see where Herbert Spencer and the Agnostics of our day get their views and their nomenclature. They deny that they are sceptics, and that they do not believe in a reality of things; but then they affirm that the nature of things cannot be known by us. Mr. Spencer thinks that there is a God, but then he is unknown and must ever be unknowable by man.

Kant draws the distinction between phenomenon and

noumenon, — between the thing appearing and the *Ding
an Sich*, the thing in itself, or, as Dr. Mahaffy translates
it, *the thing per se*. The distinction will come before us
once and again. It is an altogether unsatisfactory one.
We cannot know that a thing exists without knowing
something about it, without knowing it under the aspect
in which it makes its existence known to us.[1] In sense-
perception we know not only that the thing before us,
say that book, exists, but we know it in part; we know
it as a colored surface. We are certainly not omniscient;
we do not know all about any one thing, about ourselves,
or other things. But we know what we know, know so
much of the thing, not, it may be, of the thing in itself,
which is meaningless, as a thing cannot be in itself, but
of the thing, the very thing. In denying this, which he
does, Kant is undermining realism, and leaving us in the
darkness of nihilism.

IV.

3. In ÆSTHETIC and ANALYTIC he *makes us perceive
things, not as they are, but as made or modified by forms
in the mind.*

First, our perceptions or intuitions by the senses and
by self - consciousness come to us under the forms of
Space and Time, — Space being the form of the bodily
senses, and Time being the form both of the external and
internal senses. We are not to look on these two forms,
Space and Time, as having any objective existence, any
independent or real being. They are forms in the mind
imposed on what we perceive. It follows that we do
not and cannot know the world without us, nor even the
internal self as it is. We perceive everything as through

---

[1] I have all along been insisting on this. It is confirmed by Zeller. See *Appendix C*.

stained, and it may be twisted glass, which gives its color and form to what comes under our notice. At this point Kant's idealism enters, and it runs on through the whole of his philosophy, till, as we shall see, it culminates in pure idealism. In opposition, Realism holds that Space and Time, as well as the things contained in them, are realities, and are what we intuitively perceive them. We know matter — so much of matter; we know mind — so much of mind; and we also know space and time, in which matter and mind are — so much of space and time. As having such a knowledge, we believe in the mathematical truths derived from them by legitimate inference. If we allow, with Kant, that they are not objective realities, we shall be constrained by logic to hold that the things perceived, body and mind, are also ideal. We notice a *body* in *space* and an *event* in *time*, and we have the same evidence, an immediate evidence, of the existence of all four, the body, the space, the event, and time.

Secondly, the mind begins with the perceptions of sense, and then the understanding pronounces judgments upon these. The judgments are pronounced according to mental forms called Categories. Great pains are taken to show how these Categories are deduced. They are very much the same as the judgments of the Aristotelian or Formal Logic, of which Kant was professor: —

I. QUANTITY:

Unity,
Plurality,
Totality.

II. QUALITY:

Reality,
Negation,
Limitation.

III. RELATION:

Inherence and Subsistence,
Causality and Dependence,
Reciprocity of Agent and
Patient.

IV. MODALITY:

Possibility and Impossibility,
Existence and Non-Existence,
Necessity and Contingence.

I am not concerned to examine these forms, or determine whether they are the best possible classification of
judgments. Modern logic makes the judgments fewer.
But they have been made greatly more scientifically correct by the criticism of Kant. Here, however, our inquiry is simply, Have we come nearer to actuality? On
the contrary, we have gone farther away from it. We
have subjected what we know of it to a farther modify-
ing process. These Categories, which are all merely subjective, impose themselves upon the concepts which have
been formed by space and time being imposed on the sensibility. The place allotted to the Real seems to me to
be very artificial and awkward. He does not place it in
Æsthetics, or the domain of the senses; we do not immediately perceive it. He places it in Analytic, under
judgment. The Real which he reaches is a mere form
in the mind, not implying anything objective out of the
mind. Taking this view, the tendency of the German
philosophy has been ever towards idealism. Even the
sensationalists among them, in reducing all our powers
to sensation, do not regard our sensations as giving us a
knowledge of things.

One of the Categories is Cause and Effect. It obliges
us to look on every event as having a cause, but this does
not prove that it really has a cause; we can be assured
of this only by the experience of sense, which cannot rise
above what we experience, and cannot therefore give us
any universal truth. We would prove that a God exists
arguing from the world, which is a visible effect, — "a
manufactured article," as Sir John Herschel expresses
it, — to a cause in God. But the argument is invalid, as
we are not allowed to assert that causation is universal.
As Hume argues, we are not entitled, from causation in
our limited experience, to infer a causation in world-mak-

ing, which is beyond our experience. The same may be said of all the twelve Categories, as unity, as existence, as necessity; they carry no weight beyond the experience of sense. It thus appears that ÆSTHETIC, or the science of the senses, does not give us things as they are; that ANALYTIC, or the science of the understanding, takes us farther away from things; and we have now to turn to DIALECTIC, which inquires what reality there is in these processes of sense and understanding.

V.

In the Æsthetic and Analytic, Kant is building up: starting with phenomena formulated by Space and Time, and going on to the Categories, or the various forms of logical judgment. Under the head of Dialectics, he inquires what validity there is in the structure which he has reared.

Rising above Sense, rising above Understanding, the mind can form Ideas of Pure Reason, as he calls them. These are Substance, the Interdependence of Phenomena, and God. These Ideas give us a Rational Psychology, a Rational Cosmology, and God. We feel now as if a domain were thrown open to us wide and pure as heaven itself. We hasten to enter it, and hope that we have here a lasting possession where we can abide forever, and hold communion with the loftiest thoughts. But Kant proceeds to tell us that this grand scene is a mirage.

Kant is too powerful a logician not to see, and too honest a man not to admit, that these Forms of Sense and Categories of the Understanding cannot give us known and objective existence. He uses stronger language than I have done in expounding his system, in showing that neither sense nor understanding can reveal reality. They do not profess to give it to us: they cannot give it, for they do not themselves have it. Hitherto he has been rearing an edifice, stone upon stone, all of Cyclopean dimensions. Now the giant takes as much pains to pull it down. The constructive work is ended; the destructive work begins. As Hamilton puts it, the intellectual Samson pulls down the house upon himself.

As to Substance, we have an Idea of it, and it seems to stablish us; but it is only a form in the mind. He examines Descartes' fundamental argument, " *Cogito ergo sum.*" If the *ego* be in the *cogito*, it is all a mere assumption; if it is not in the *cogito*, we cannot put it in the conclusion without having more in the conclusion than in the premises.

As to the Interdependence of Phenomena, he labors to prove that, on the supposition that phenomena are facts and not mere forms, we are landed in a succession of contradictions or Antinomies. As an example, we are led, on the one hand, to hold that the world has a beginning in time, and, on the other, that it has had no beginning in time. For myself, I hold that pure Reason alone cannot establish either of these positions; but Kant holds that it can prove both, and that the two counteract each other and leave us only zero.

As to the Idea of God, we are obliged to contemplate Him theoretically, but we can prove his existence only on the principle of cause and effect; but we have no evidence that this is universal, and so the argument is not conclusive. Speculatively there is a God, logically and really there is no proof of the existence of God.

Let us realize the position to which we have been brought. Let us see where we stand, on rock or quagmire. In Sense we have some reality in phenomena which are subjective, but imply an external reality. In Understanding we have less reality, but we have subjective Categories binding the appearances. In Reason we have only the ghosts of departed realities. Our inheritance does not consist of coins, but only of paper currency with no guarantee behind.

It might seem as if in being led to do all this work, and passing through all these difficult passages, we had been deprived of our promised wages. But Kant denies this, and reminds us that he has never given us any assurance of our finding reality. There is no deception, for there has been no promise. But he admits fully and proclaims decidedly that there is *Illusion*. We all fall naturally and necessarily into the illusion, just as when we stand on the shore we see the ocean level and not rounded ; just as when we look up into the sky we see it as a vault and not an expanse.

VI.

Kant calls in Moral Reason to save us from the nescience of the speculative Reason. This Moral Reason announces a fundamental law: it is expressed in the Categorical Imperative (an admirable phrase), and is simply a modification of our Lord's supreme law, " Do unto others as ye would that they should do unto you." It is, " Act according to a rule which might be applied to all intelligences." This implies that man is free, and as a corollary that he is responsible; that there is a judgment day, and therefore a future life, and a God to guarantee the whole. Morality, immortality, and God are thus bound up together.

I think that Kant means us to understand that he has here reached reality. The moral law and its corollaries,

freedom, responsibility, and a judgment day, are all
actual existences. He thus held resolutely by great
truths which preserve us from scepticism, and lead the
way to and guarantee other truths. I am inclined to
think that he meant these moral truths to sanction the
validity of the truths of the speculative reason, specially
the existence of responsible beings who are under the
moral law. He thus counteracts by his moral principles
the nescience of his speculative principles. Viewed
under this aspect, the tendency of his philosophy is all
for good.

However, it has been doubted whether he can reach
and retain an independent moral reason in consistency
with his speculative nescience. The nescient principle
carried out logically, seems to bear against the moral
reason quite as much as the speculative reason. How
does moral perception come in? He says that the senses
alone have the power of intuition which he denies to the
Reason. But if the reason have no power of intuition,
how can we come to discern and appreciate moral good?
If it comes in by the gate of sense, shaped by the Categories and idealized by pure reason, then we are landed
in nescience by the moral reason as we are by the speculative reason. Whatever may be Kant's doctrine on this
subject, it is evident that his moral law, if it has any
meaning, must apply to living beings who are supposed
to be under it; but we can know that there are such
beings only through the forms of sense, the Categories
of the understanding, and the ideas of pure reason; and
these he shows are illusions. I do not see how he can
logically reach the reality of the moral power, or the
corollary which he derives from it, the existence of God.
From ideal, that is, illusory premises, we can draw only
ideal and illusory conclusions. From ideal facts we can

infer only an ideal God: this in truth seems to be all that some of the theologies of Germany have.

It has been urged all along — ever since the publication of the "Kritik" — that Kant is inconsistent in standing up for the reality of the moral, and denying that of the speculative reason. I believe that both stand on the same foundation, which is a foundation of reality. But, whether consistently or inconsistently, Kant has done immeasurable good by standing up so resolutely for the reality and validity of the Moral Reason.

VII.

I may notice here the tendency for the last few ages to acknowledge that the intelligence of man leads to infidelity, from which we may be saved by Faith or Feeling. This style of speaking was derived from Kant and Jacobi, and has been adopted by many German, British, and American thinkers. They tell us, with a sigh, often of affectation, that the understanding leads to scepticism, and then, with Jacobi, call in faith to lift them out of the slough. I do not believe that there is any such schism in the mind which God has made in his own image. I deny that one part of our nature contradicts another. I deny that the understanding, following its laws, issues logically in scepticism. I am sure that he who thinks that intelligence ends in scepticism will not be brought back to truth by a loose appeal to faith. The sceptic who has attacked the validity of reason, having tasted blood, will, on a like principle, attack the trustworthiness of faith. I am sure that intelligence and faith both reveal truth to us, each in its own way; the one of things that are seen, the other of things that are not seen.

In the philosophy of Kant there are two powerful but discordant elements, the ideal and the nescient, each of which has produced its proper effect. The ideal ran its course in the first instance; passing through Fichte and Schelling, and culminating in Hegel, being pantheistic throughout. I do not wonder that Kant, who wished to be regarded as a realist, was offended with Fichte, who seized certain of his principles and followed them out to a pure idealism. Schelling worked to correct the one-sidedness of Fichte, and brought in object as well as subject; but made the two identical and both subjective, so that he can have no objective reality. And what shall I say of Hegel? He has dived down into depths and mounted into heights to which I cannot follow him, and in which human logic, as it appears to me, has no place. When I find that he employs his *a-priori* powers to set aside the demonstration of Newton, that he holds Being and Not-Being as identical, that Being and Thinking are the same, and that contradictories may both be true, I regard his system as a *reductio ad absurdum* of the whole of his philosophy. I have heard in Berlin an eminent professor of his school proving to his own satisfaction that all is one: that you and I, God and Nature, mind and body, truth and error, good and evil, are all one. In his all-comprehensive system, which embraces everything, he has a reality claimed by him, but it is a reality merely in his *a-priori* forms. He would turn away with disdain from the reality which I am pleading for, and which insists that we intuitively know things as they are.

VIII.

Upward of two hundred works have been published in Germany, besides dozens in other countries, on the philosophy of Kant, who has been almost deified for one hundred years by his followers, as Aristotle was deified for five hundred years in mediæval times. Most of the works are liable to the objections which I have taken to Kant. There are some, however, who are longing for reality in philosophy, and, perceiving that Kant has not furnished it, have endeavored to discover it by a course of their own. But they have been so bound as by cords with the forms of Kant, that they have not been able to break forth into full and independent liberty.

In seeking to avoid the extremes to which Hegel led his admirers, there has been a loud cry of "Back to Kant!" I believe this to be a wiser course than to go on with Hegel or beyond him. Kant's Kritik is, after all, a more consistent structure than that of any of his followers. In many of his logical analyses, and in his ethical principles, he has expounded truths on which the mind may rest in the assurance that it will never be moved. But should philosophy be brought back to the position of Kant, being in a state of unstable equilibrium, it will run on in one or other of the courses which Kantism has hitherto followed, either with idealism or agnosticism; or, more probably, with an incongruous mixture of the two which will not amalgamate.

In examining the New Kantian School I have fallen in with a work by Stählen, which seems to me to state and review the more eminent systems of that school fairly and searchingly, and I take advantage of the criticism urged.[1]

There is Lange, author of a learned and elaborate work, "History of Materialism." This is esteemed by the New Kantians as the most philosophic performance

---

[1] *Kant, Lotze, and Ritschel,* by Leonhard Stählen, translated by D. W. Simon, Ph. D.

of the present day. The author is regarded as an apostle
of the Kantian view of the world, and the leader of the
new movement. Says Stählen: "It is decidedly and at
once significant of the direction which Lange's thought
takes, that he sets aside the realistic factor which Kant's
theory of knowledge endeavored to retain." " The thing
in itself is simply a limitative or regulative conception.
We do not know whether things in themselves exist."
"His own presuppositions leave him no alternative but
to teach that the entire phenomenal world, as well as the
organs by means of which it is apprehended, are a product of our representation."

There is Lotze, whose instructions have been attended
by so many English and Americans as well as Germans.
He has a kind of reality. He assumed " the existence of ʹ
an infinite multiplicity of simple beings which constitute
the basis of the world of sense, and, after Herbart's example, designates them the Reals. In Lotze's view, these
same Reals are of the nature of souls, spirits, because of
their independent existence." Surely all this is a speculative fancy, which explains nothing, and of the existence
of which we have no proof from sense or consciousness.
"What, then, becomes of the world of sense? It is a
mere phenomenon ; and not even objective phenomenon,
but phenomenal in a purely subjective sense." Space
and Time are ideal. "But if space is a mere form of
subjective intuition, that which we intuite in space is as
exclusively in us as space itself; outside of us there is
nothing. Time also, in like manner, is a form of intuition ; the temporal-spatial world itself is phenomenal."
He proceeds a step farther. "According to Lotze, the
being of things is a standing in relations. It is of the
very idea and essence of that which exists to stand in
relations ; there is no such thing as existence without

relations; there is no other sort of actual existence but
the standing in relations."

Stähzen seems to be justified in his strong statements.
" The corner-stone of the Kritik of Reason is, we do not
know even ourselves as we are in ourselves, but merely
as we appear to ourselves." He concludes: " The edifice
of the Kantian philosophy has fallen in ruins before our
eyes, crushed beneath the weight of its own contradictions; and even the ruins themselves have disappeared
in a bottomless pit. In so far, therefore, the result of the
critical system is null. We have seen that it cannot possibly be the system of truth; that, on the contrary, the
consequences are utter illusion and nihilism."

While Kant had a strong ideal element, he had an
equally strong — in the end a stronger — nescient element. It is affirmed that the mind begins with phenomena in the sense of appearances, and can never know
things as they are, either without or within us; in fact,
either body or mind. This view, as we shall see immediately, was adopted so far by Hamilton, and from him
has been taken up by a powerful speculator who has the
advantage of a large acquaintance — as an amateur —
with physical science, who argues powerfully that things
exist, but with equal power that we can never know their
nature. We see now how it is that Agnosticism is so
prevalent; is, in fact, the prevalent heresy of our day.
Professor Huxley, President of the Royal Society of
London, who sits in the chair of Newton and has adopted
the scepticism of Hume, and Mr. Spencer, who is so influential a thinker, have brought us to this blank issue.
Agnosticism is in the air, and our young men are obliged
to breathe it as they read the pages of many of our
popular journals. Not that the writers or readers are
able to follow the concatenated reasoning of Kant,

Hamilton, and Spencer; but they catch the results, and carry them out to their practical consequences.

But our souls cannot live in this void any more than our bodies can live in a vacuum, and there must soon be a rush out of this confined, this dark and damp malarial cellar, into the free and open, the pure and healthy air, where we can live and breathe, walk and run.

SECTION EIGHTH.

I.

THIS school has not so much influence now as it had at the end of the last century and the beginning of this, when it was the only philosophy taught in Scotland, and had large power in France where it met the prevailing sensational philosophy, and when it was expounded in most of the colleges of the United States. In Scotland it has able and independent supporters, though Kant and Hegel divide the dominion with it. In France and the United States it has a traditional influence for good, where its sound and safe principles are taught by many professors, who are unaware of the source from which they have drawn them.

The founder of the school was Francis Hutcheson, who, in general philosophy, held with Locke that all that is perceived by the mind are ideas; but Shaftesbury brought in a number of other senses besides the sensation and reflection of Locke, such as the moral sense and the sense of honor. The true representative of the school is Thomas Reid, a careful observer, a sincere lover of truth, an independent thinker, carefully avoiding all rash speculations. He had two great ends in view in all his writings. The one was, to lay down principles in opposition to his contemporary, David Hume, who was undermining all natural and moral truth; the other end was, to overthrow and set aside Locke's theory of ideas, which seemed to him to come between the mind and things, and thus to be the main support of the scepticism of Hume.

II.

To accomplish the first of these ends, he called in Common Sense. The phrase and the doctrine are defended by the erudition of Sir W. Hamilton; but they are somewhat ambiguous. Besides its Aristotelian meaning, where it denotes the percepts common to all the senses, it has two meanings in conversation and in literature: it may signify good sense or sound judgment in the affairs of life — said to be the most uncommon of all the senses — or, the principles of thought and belief common to all men. It is only in this latter sense that it can be used in philosophy. Less ambiguous phrases may be employed to denote this last quality, say " fundamental laws of thought and belief," employed by Reid's disciple, Dugald Stewart. Thus expressed, it may be maintained that the doctrine of Reid and his school met Hume more satisfactorily than Kant did with his greater logical power.

To accomplish his second point, Reid gives what he regards as the true account of sense-perception. He argues most conclusively that we cannot arrive at a knowledge of the external world by reasoning. He unfolds what he regards as the mental process in sense-perception. There is first a sensation produced by the external object; then there is a perception suggested instinctively by the sensation. The *instinctive suggestion* seems to me to be as little satisfactory as the idea of Locke. He does not give the mind, with Aristotle, a knowing or gnostic power. It is thus by an indirect or mediate process that we reach reality. It does not appear that the mind can directly perceive; that is, know the thing.

He further holds that we do not perceive things, but only the qualities of things, which imply the existence of things. This doctrine is not announced so openly by Reid, but is emphatically declared by Dugald Stewart. Neither has expressed the true doctrine, which is, that we perceive things, the very things, by sense-perception. We perceive things by their qualities.

III.

Sir William Hamilton is the most erudite of the Scottish metaphysicians. In this respect he is worthy of being put alongside of the great German scholars. He gives us quotations, with critical strictures, from obscure writers of various ages and countries. In all his discussions he uses a sharp, two-edged sword. He was brought up in the school of Reid, and boldly defended him when the younger metaphysicians were beginning to assail him because of his caution. In his lectures on Logic and Metaphysics, afterward published, he travels far beyond the narrow field cultivated by the Scottish School. He has made very valuable contributions, and thrown out very definite opinions in regard to all the mental sciences, except, perhaps, Ethics, which he does not seem to have specially studied.

IV.

The Scottish School generally, especially Dugald Stewart, give a high place to moral perceptions. In this respect they are all realists, except Thomas Brown, who makes virtue consist in mere feelings. None of them allows that the mind is capable of rising to a positive idea of infinity. Hamilton argues powerfully, with British philosophers generally, that our idea of infinity is merely negative, though he seems to allow that, while we have no positive idea of infinity, we have a faith in it, — as if we could believe in a thing of which we have no idea. Surely there must be some way of showing that, as we think and talk intelligently about infinity, eternity, omniscience, we must have some positive though necessarily inadequate idea of it. I maintain that we have an idea of something that is beyond our widest concept, and is such that nothing can be added to it.

We have here to do simply with the relation of Hamilton's philosophy to Realism. He professes throughout to be a realist. Those things we immediately perceive are the real things. "The material reality is the object immediately known in perception." "The very things which we perceive by our senses do really exist."[1] But he studied the philosophy of Kant, with which very few Scotchmen were at that time acquainted, and, perceiving the common points of agreement between the Scotch and German schools, he sought to combine them. But they will not coalesce. Hamilton reached and expounded a doctrine which seems to me to conflict with the realism of Reid. He adopted and defended with great logical ability the doctrine of Relativity. "Our knowledge is relative, first, because existence is not cognizable absolutely and in itself, but only in special modes; second, because these modes thus relative to our faculties are presented to and known by the mind, only under modification, determined by these faculties themselves."[2] My readers will notice that here we have thoroughly Kantian principles, which cannot be grafted on the realist stock. In the three general propositions, and in the sev-

---

[1] *Met.*, vol. i. pp. 279, 289.   [2] *Met.*, vol. i. p. 148.

eral clauses, there are an immense number and variety
of assertions wrapped up. Some are commonly enter-
tained, but others are joined on to them, from which I
strongly dissent. I acknowledge, first, as self-evident,
that things are known only as we have the capacity to
know them; and this is limited. I acknowledge, secondly, that we do not know all things; nay, that we do
not know all about any one thing. In other words, that
our knowledge is partial or finite, as distinguished from
perfect or absolute. I may admit, thirdly, that man dis-
covers internal objects only under a relation to himself
and his cognitive powers. So much I allow. But, on
the other hand, I demur, first, to the Kantian statement,
that we do not know existence in itself, or, as he expresses it elsewhere, that we do not know the thing in
itself (*Ding an Sich*). I do not like this language: it is
ambiguous; when thoroughly sifted it is meaningless. I
doubt much whether there can be such a thing as "existence in itself," and of course what does not exist cannot
be known. If he means that we do not know things as
existing, I deny the statement. Everything we know we
know as existing; not only so, but we know the thing
itself; not all about the thing, but so much of the very
thing. Then I demur, secondly, to the statement which
is thoroughly Kantian, that the mind in cognition adds
elements of its own. As Hamilton expresses it: "Suppose that the total object of consciousness = 12; and
that the external reality contributes 6, the material sense
3, and the mind 3. This may enable you to form some
rude conjecture of the nature of the object of perception." [1] To suppose that in perception or cognition the
mind adds anything, is a doctrine fraught with destructive consequences; for, if it adds one thing, why not two

[1] *Met.*, vol. ii. p. 129.

things, or ten things, or all things, till we are left in absolute idealism, which means absolute nihilism?

Hamilton is logical enough and candid enough to admit the issue. Comparing his philosophy with that of
Germany, he says: " Extremes meet. In one respect
both coincide, for both agree that the knowledge of nothing is the principle or consummation of all true philosophy, — *Scire nihil; studium quo nos laetamer utrique.*"
But the one doctrine, openly maintaining that nothing
must yield everything, is a philosophic omniscience;
whereas the other, holding that nothing can yield nothing, is a philosophic nescience. In other words, the doctrine of the unconditioned is a philosophy confessing
relative ignorance, but professing absolute knowledge;
while the doctrine of the conditioned (Hamilton's doctrine) is a philosophy professing relative knowledge, but
confessing absolute ignorance." [1]   I confess I always feel
chilled when I read this passage.

Hamilton's learned follower in Oxford, Dr. Mansel,
in his famous Bampton Lectures, used his principles to
undermine Rationalism in religion ; but in so doing he
undermined, without meaning it, religion itself, as he
did not leave to us those great truths of Nature which
conduct us to revealed religion.

Sir James Mackintosh and Dr. Chalmers, who were
trained in the Scottish school, were greatly delighted
when, in their later life, they discovered the close resem-
blance of the German and Scottish philosophies. The
two agree in standing up for what the one called *a-priori*
and the other fundamental principles. But while they
agree they also differ. The main difference is, that in
discovering what these principles are, the one proceeds
in the Critical and the other in the Inductive method.

[1] *Discussions*, p. 609.

The one discards observation; the other uses it, not indeed as the foundation of first truths, but as the means of discovering them. I am trying to give the proper place to the induction which is so recommended by Reid, Stewart, and Chalmers, and which is fitted to keep philosophy from the extravagances into which it is so apt to fall, and which can be corrected only by its being ever compelled to fall back on facts and the observation of facts. Just as logic is an expression of the processes of the mind in discursive thought, so is metaphysics the expression of what passes in the mind in discerning primary truth. The exact expression is reached in both cases in a careful observation of the mind in the respective operations.

SECTION NINTH.

THE SENSATIONAL SCHOOL.

Sensationalism had already appeared in the philosophy of Thomas Hobbes, who derived all our ideas and knowledge from sensation, and allowed that we could never reach a spiritual reality in man or God. But what is specially called the sensational school originated with Condillac, who left out the Reflection of Locke, took no notice of his power of Intuition, and represented all our ideas, even the highest, as " transformed sensations."

In Great Britain the school has had a series of able men holding by Sensationalism, in James Mill, John Stuart Mill, G. H. Lewes, Alexander Bain, and in part Herbert Spencer. All of these have proceeded more or less fully on the negative and sceptical principles of David Hume.

We may take JOHN STUART MILL as the representative British sensationalist, as he sees more clearly than any other the logical consequences of the system, and is candid enough to admit and defend them. Body is defined by him as the " possibility of sensations," and mind as " a series of feelings aware of itself." [1] Almost every intelligent reader has felt this to be a very scanty remnant of the knowledge which we thought we had of ourselves, and of the persons and objects around us.

[1] *Exam. of Hamilton*, and my work, *Exam. of Mill*.

Most people have felt it to be a *reductio ad absurdum* of the whole system. Naturally we think that we have more than this in body and mind; that we perceive body as having extension and a power of resistance; that we are conscious of mind as having intelligence and moral perception. But Mr. Mill is a clear and candid reasoner, and these are the legitimate results of the sensational system. You can get something higher, say personality and intelligence and conscience only by introducing them from without, surreptitiously to clothe the nakedness of the system.

GEORGE HENRY LEWES holds the doctrine of Reasoned Realism.[1] He admits that " the ordinary man believes that the objects he sees, touches, and tastes do veritably exist, and exist as they are seen, touched, tasted." This doctrine is at once rejected. His system is Realism, " because it affirms the reality of what is given in feeling; and Reasoned Realism, because it justifies that affirmation through the ground and processes of philosophy, when philosophy explains the facts given in Feeling." Observe here that feeling is all in all. " The reality of an external existence, Not-self, is a fact of Feeling; Knowledge in all its manifold varieties is a classification of virtual feelings." His general conclusion is: " Mind is a form or function of Life." The Moral Sense consists of certain organized predispositions that spontaneously or docilely issue in the beneficent forms of action, which the experience of society has classed as right." Surely this is a very meagre account of the high qualities of which we are directly conscious in mind.

ALEXANDER BAIN says: " Mind possesses three attributes or capacities: (1) It has Feeling, in which I

[1] *Problems of Life and Mind*, pp. 263, 287.

include what is conveniently called Sensation and Emotion. (2) It can act according to Feeling. (3) It can think." Consciousness is the same attribute of mind as "Feeling and Emotion." Thinking consists in discovering Difference and Agreement, and in Retentiveness; and it proceeds by the laws of Contiguity and Similarity. The Moral Faculty is resolved into "Prudence, Sympathy, and Emotions generally." In this list of man's powers we miss those which raise him above this world and ally him to God. In regard to the independent existence of body his language is ambiguous. "There is no possible knowledge of the world except in reference to our minds. Knowledge means a state of mind." The latter clause is correct. The former may mean that we know matter simply as related to us, whereas we know it with qualities of extension and force, as having an existence independent of our existence. Mind and matter are not at all carefully distinguished; they are represented as the opposite sides of the same thing, as if the soul, which is spiritual, could have a side except in a metaphorical sense.[1]

In France, where Sensationalism so prevailed at the end of last century, it may suffice to look to H. TAINE, the present representative of the system. He makes Intelligence to consist largely of names, images, and ideas. He reduces ideas to a class of images, and images to a class of sensations. Names are a class of images. The laws of ideas bring back the laws of images. Mind is an aggregate (*polypier*) of images. In itself, external perception is a true hallucination. We have found that the objects that we call body are only internal phantoms; that is, the fragments of one detached from them

---

[1] *Mental and Moral Science*, pp. 1, 8, 24, 250, 433; *Senses and Intellect*, p. 250.

in appearance and opposed to them, while in reality they themselves are the self under another aspect. So much for body, which he makes so illusory. As to moral personality, that which makes the continuity of a distinct person, it is the continued renaissance of the same group of distinct images.[1]

It may seem as if sensationalism is a very inoffensive, as it is a very simple, creed. But, if truly believed in, it arrests the growth of all higher aims and aspirations, moral and spiritual.

In closing this survey I may refer to TH. RIBOT, who has given us many valuable facts as to the relation of mind and body, but as a philosopher is a sensationalist, undermining in his journal that high school of philosophers who appeared in France in the second quarter of this century, including Cousin, Saisset, Simon, and others.

In this criticism, I have been looking at the men solely in regard to their ability to find actuality. Locke was personally a believer in things without us, as we naturally apprehend them; but could get no proof of their existence, as he held that the mind can perceive only its own ideas. Of the sensationalists proper, some have no other reality than sensations or feelings modified and transformed, and have not reached and cannot reach things without or within us. None of them have a belief in man's personality and continued identity as evidenced in memory. None of them can rise to truth beyond experience, to truth necessary and universal. None of them acknowledge that we perceive immediately moral good, or that we can stand up for an immutable and eternal morality.

Meanwhile two formidable men have appeared to carry out the empirical doctrine to its logical results.

---

[1] Taine, *De l'Intelligence.*

Professor Huxley expounds and defends the doctrine of Hume slightly modified. He represents the mind as having Impressions, which he divides into — A, sensations; B, pleasure and pain; C, relations between these. This is a very meagre account of the furniture of the mind.

SECTION TENTH.

HUXLEY AND HERBERT SPENCER.

AT this place Spencer comes in. It is evident that he is much swayed by, and started from the position of Hamilton and Mansel, whose philosophy was the reigning one in Great Britain at that time. Many think, and I agree with them, that he followed out their doctrine to its logical conclusion. I do not see that Hamilton's principles can stop short of the agnosticism of which Spencer is the ablest expounder. I pressed Dr. Mansel to meet this downward current, but he never did so, and Hamilton's pupils have not done so. He is the most powerful philosophic speculator of our day. He would discuss every subject connected with the operations and laws of nature and answer every question. I have sometimes thought that at times he speculated beyond the capacity of the human intellect. He does not proceed in the slow and cautious way of observation recommended by Francis Bacon; but by the power of thought rises at once to the highest laws, and draws from them a long line of consequences.

I would not charge him with being an out and out defender of nescience or agnosticism. In certain places he argues most powerfully for the existence of objects. But then these objects are in their very nature unknown and unknowable to us.

He argues resolutely the existence of God, but then
God is unknown and unknowable by man. He identi-
fies him with the unknown God to whom the Apostle
Paul saw an altar dedicated. Now, both the human head
and the human heart require a God so far known, to
whom we give obedience and love. In his Psychology
he speaks in the same way of the human mind. He
argues its existence, but he denies that we know or can
know it as a faculty. He uses the very strongest language on this subject. " We know nothing about it and
never can know anything about it. Is it not enough to
say that such knowledge is beyond the path of human
intelligence as it now exists, for no amount of what we
call intelligence, however transcendent, can grasp such
knowledge." He tells us that "a nervous shock is the
ultimate unit of consciousness ; and that all the unlike-
ness among our feelings result from unlike modes of this
ultimate unit." (Spencer's Psych.) I confess I have
an extreme aversion to this phrase "nervous shock"
as used by Spencer and Bain to express mental action.
Apparently he can get no farther than Hume the sceptic,
who made mind consist of impressions and ideas. He
declares formally and emphatically, " Mind being composed of Feelings and the relations between Feelings
and the aptitudes of Feelings for entering into Relations
varying with their kinds." (Psych.) What! What, is
this all he can make of man's intellectual talents, of his
philosophic talent, of his mathematical, of his artistic, of
his mechanical talents, of his sagacity on the practical
affairs of life. Surely these are as prominent as our
feelings and have as much right to be included in our
mental powers.

SECTION ELEVENTH.

REALISM AND RELIGION.

THE Realistic view, as the true one, is the one most favorable to religion, which proceeds on facts and not on phenomena in the sense of appearances. Thus, when it says: Rom. i. 20 : " For the invisible things of God from the creation of the world are clearly seen, being understood by the things that are made, even his eternal power and godhead," where both "the invisible things of God " and "the things that are made " are facts and not mere phenomena. The same may be said of such passages as these: " Rejoice with them that do rejoice and weep with them that weep." All such passages refer to facts and not to vague appearances, and carry with them our convictions and our confidence.

In Germany they follow Kant and regard what we discern and what is revealed to us in Scripture as phenomena, that is, as appearances. The view which they take is in consequence pliable and insecure, first in their philosophy and then in their theology as swayed by their philosophy. These views fermenting in Germany come over into Great Britain and America and trouble our theology and our students.

SECTION TWELFTH.

I.

AT the close we may take a look backward at the ground over which we have traveled.

EXPERIENTIAL PHILOSOPHY cannot give us universal or necessary truth, or any truth beyond the narrow limits of observation. It is doubtful whether it can furnish a valid argument for the existence of God. In the system of Locke we are supposed to perceive only ideas, and are precluded from the knowledge of things.

SENSATIONALISM gives us sensations and feelings variously compounded, and we cannot from these derive mind or even body as substances, but only, as Mill concludes, "possibilities of sensation" and "a series of feelings aware of itself."

THE A-PRIORI SCHOOL OF KANT makes our first perceptions to be of phenomena (appearances) and not of things. Then all that we know has *Forms* imposed upon it by the subjective mind, so that, while we must believe in the existence of things, we do not know what they are. We pronounce judgments upon them, but according to the restrictive laws of subjective *Categories*. The result is, that, when we would argue the existence of substance, cause, and other connections, and of God, we find ourselves in a world of *Illusions*. A vigorous attempt is made to save us from nescience by calling in Moral Rea-

on, which gives us a high idea of duty, of a judgment
day, and of God, which are all real; but it is doubtful
whether the system can legitimately give us a known
world of things to which to apply them. It is evident
that an ideal world can give us only an ideal or pantheistic God.

THE SCOTTISH SCHOOL proposes to be, means to be,
and professes to be realist; but in the pages of Reid and
Stewart it speaks doubtfully about our perceiving things,
and in the pages of Hamilton it gives us only relative
knowledge, which is not a knowledge of things as they
are, and ends avowedly in nescience.

II.

I have shown that Hamilton was led into agnosticism by the critical philosophy of Kant; and Mansel
applied this doctrine to overthrow rationalism. It was
when Hamilton and Mansel were in the ascendant that
Herbert Spencer began to think and write on these
subjects, and drove the prevailing doctrine to agnosticism. He argues powerfully that we are constrained to
believe that things exist; but he maintains as resolutely
that we do not and cannot know the nature of things.
It can be shown, as I have done in various parts of my
works, that we cannot know that things exist except we
know so much of their nature.[1] Without this, any predication of their nature would be meaningless; it would
be a predication about something unknown, and we could
have no apprehension of what the predication referred to.
This is the position to which Kant and Hamilton have
brought us, and it is now occupied by Mr. Spencer: that
things exist, but that we do not and cannot know their

[1] See *Appendix C.*

nature. Spencer shows that, while we have sensations, which are simply affections of the nerves, and can pronounce judgments upon them, we have, and can have, no insight into what they are.

III.

If there be any truth, even partial truth, in this representation, philosophy has come to a crisis, such as it did when Berkeley drove the partial idealism of Descartes and Locke to pure idealism, and Hume drove the whole school to nihilism. Speculations have thus been shown to be false by the consequences to which they lead. The vessel has foundered because it has not followed the right track. The train has been wrecked by the bursting of the materials which it carries. As philosophy has inflicted the wound, it must hasten to heal it. It must begin to build anew (for the human head, not to speak of the human heart, will not be satisfied with an agnostic philosophy) ; and it will have this advantage, that the ground has been so far cleared of incumbrances. I trust it will rise as a phœnix from its ashes, profiting by the blunders it has made, and purified by the fires through which it has passed.

Realism is the one thing to be introduced into modern philosophy (it will be shown that it had a place, though not always the right place, in the ancient Greek philosophy) to give it coherence and consistency. Philosophy, whatever else it may do, aims at settling foundations. But reality is the firmest of all foundations. A chink has appeared in the wall, indicating that there is some insecurity at the base. There are crevices staring us in the face, and they have to be filled up. We may find that these evils can be remedied by giving reality its proper place in the rock on which the building stands, and in the cement which binds the parts together. In this process some abutments which are incumbrances will require to be taken down; but the edifice will rest more firmly upon its well-laid foundation.

We see how it is that Agnosticism is so prevalent in the present day. Young men, pondering a deep subject in religion, in morals, or science, with which they are troubled, find that philosophy, with all its professions and pretensions, gives them little to rest on in the last resort; and they conclude that nothing can be known as it is. Those who would confute this Agnosticism experience great difficulty in doing so. The reason is, that they have no ground, no ποῦ στῶ, on which to stand. They commonly satisfy themselves with proving, which they can do easily and successfully, that nescience is suicidal. It is an evident contradiction to affirm that we know that we can know nothing. But they do not see that in establishing this point they are only playing into the hands of the agnostics. For by far the most powerful argument of Hume and the sceptics is, that there are contradictions, antinomies (as they call them), in our nature, and so conclude that human reason cannot be trusted. They set two strong contradictory propositions before us that counteract and arrest each other, and leave nothing between. Many an ambitious youth is laboring to pull down Mr. Spencer's imposing structure only to find it falling on himself. He propounds an argument which seems profound; but, on searching it, it is seen to assume the reality which he proposed to prove. The only successful method of meeting Agnosticism is to assume reality; not trying to prove it, but taking it for granted, as we do the axioms of geometry as an intuitive truth, which can stand the tests of intuition.

IV.

It is acknowledged on all hands that we cannot prove every truth by syllogism, or by any mediate or external evidence. We can prove only by premises given and allowed. But, if we are to prove every truth, we have also to prove the premises, which have to be proven by prior premises; and thus we need an endless chain of premises hanging on each other, and the whole hanging on nothing. There are truths which do not require to be proven; they have their evidence in themselves, and we have an intuitive power of discerning it. Of this character are the axioms of geometry. No one should attempt to prove them; if any one does, he will find that the evidence he employs is not so clear and certain as the axiom itself is. We assume the axiom without seeking proof, and in doing so we are not acting unreasonably; we are assuming what we know by a higher reason than mediate reasoning. Spontaneously we are sure that we have reality in what is presented to us by the senses and by self-consciousness. I believe that this is the first truth which the infant mind knows as it wakes into existence. Being so, philosophy should take it up and start with it; it should not attempt to demonstrate it. If any one is not satisfied with this statement let him try to prove his own existence. What external proof can he bring? Perhaps he may answer, Some one, my father, told me so. But does he not see that, in order to reach the existence of the father, he has to assume his own existence?

V.

I am insisting that to every philosophy the question be put, What do you make of reality? If you omit it, I demand that you give it a place; otherwise your system is a mere speculation. If you give it a place, I ask, At what place? — at the entrance? in the middle? or at the close? In this inquiry it will turn out that reality cannot be proven except by premises that contain reality, and that it is to be assumed in philosophy, even as it is taken for granted and acted upon in our native perceptions.

I am aware that in pursuing this course perplexities and difficulties will arise, as they do in all branches of investigation, physical and metaphysical; but there will be far greater difficulties in following any other course; for the reality which we have unnaturally shut out will ever be coming back to assert its existence, authority, and claims, and to disturb and confound the errors which have taken its place. It will turn out that, whatever mysteries may cast up in carrying out this assumption, there will be no positive contradictions; and the reality will hold its place when the spectres and illusions have been obliged to vanish in the light of actuality.

Of all things, it is most essential that we should know what is the precise reality which we intuitively know. This must be carefully separated, by the " necessary rejections and exclusions," from all adventitious circumstances, such as sensations and feelings.

We look through a perfectly transparent glass on a tree before us. What is it that we see? It is not the glass, but the tree; so when we take away the glass it is not the eye but the tree that we perceive. A like remark may be made of all the senses. Let us try to ascertain the precise object perceived by each of the windows of the soul.

In Sight what I perceive is not the retina and brain affection, but a colored surface. In the Muscular Sense

I do not observe the nerve which moves the muscle in locomotive action, nor the nerve which carries up the notice of the motion to the brain; I perceive merely the muscle resisted by an object.

In Touch Proper, or Feeling, we do not discern the nerve, but merely the sensitive feeling which we localize at the point which the nerve reaches.

In Hearing I am conscious, not of the tympanum, the hammer and stirrup, and other apparatus, but simply of a sound in the ear.

In Taste we know our palate as affected.   In Smell we know our nostrils as affected.

By the last four of these we know directly only what are called Secondary Qualities of body; that is, special affections of body for which we are prompted to seek a cause beyond our organic frame, as it is not in our frame, and are commonly able to find it.   By a combination of the perceptions of the primary and secondary qualities thus reached, we are able to form a knowledge of body, say of an orange : by sight, as extended, or in space and as colored; by the muscular sense, as having resisting force; by hearing, as capable of issuing sound; by touch, taste, and smell, as capable of rousing sensations of special sorts.

VII.

Having now an internal and external world, all of realities, we can add to them indefinitely by reasoning, and by the continued observations of sense and consciousness.   Thus we can know not only the shape of this triangle, but by necessary inference that its angles are equal to two right angles.   We have the moral law: " Do unto others as ye would that they should do unto you ; " but further, as a consequence that we should show kindness to this poor man, this negro, this enemy of ours, this slave, this criminal, and this infidel. We have the facts brought back by memory, the records of history, the discoveries of science. By these processes, conducted by ourselves and others whom we trust, we can increase our knowledge wide as the knowable world, and all be of realities.

But it is asked in a disdainful manner, Do you presumptuously propose to set aside all previous philosophies: that of Plato and Aristotle, of Descartes and Locke, of Kant and Reid? I answer at once and decisively, I reject none of the great truths which have been established by the great thinkers of the world, greatly to the benefit of the world. I mean simply to settle some of them upon a surer foundation. Some of them seem to me to be resting on perishable piles, like the houses in Venice; I would found them on the rock of reality. In some of them there are visible cracks and excrescences, sceptical and ideal; I would fill them up by bringing in the reality, which they have overlooked because it is so near, and put it in the room of the incumbrances. We may thus retain, and in a secure position, all that is true and good in the systems of ancient Greece and modern Europe.

VIII.

I acknowledge and claim, if the philosophy of reality is assumed, amendments will require to be made on certain of the prevailing philosophies, in the way both of addition and subtraction. Empiricists will have to take in much that they have overlooked and omitted. Along with their sensations and feelings, images and symbols, they will have to accept and embrace higher truths, such as self - personality, substance, moral obligation, which are all realities revealed by consciousness. We have as strong and quite as convincing proof of the latter of these principles as we have of the former. The Scottish School must be made to throw away its crutches of impressions, instincts, suggestions, and common sense, and give the mind a power of seeing things directly. The *a-priori* philosophy must be made to begin with things material and mental, instead of subjective laws. It must be led to regard space and time as realities quite as much as the objects we perceive in them. The Categories of the understanding must take the shape of, and be represented as, laws of the mind; such as cause and effect, which we perceive to be in the very nature of things acting. The higher ideas, such as substance, the connection of things and Deity, must be so apprehended and stated as to show that they are realities which we can know and believe in, and feel them to be the most steadfast and exalting truths which the mind can dwell on.

But it will be objected that in this realistic philosophy we seem to have no room left for idealism. I answer, that I leave to it its own province, which is one of the richest and most fertile which God has allotted to man; it is the region of imagination, with fancy and feeling to endear them to us. But we must keep idealism in its own province. We do not allow it a place in science, say in astronomy or chemistry, in social or political science. We do not permit it to attempt to improve or beautify the laws of gravitation, of animal and plant life, of the economic law of supply and demand. We insist on all these keeping rigidly to facts. We then allow idealism to come in and embellish them as it can. And the wider the sciences of fact extend their discoveries, the more extensive is the field opened to the play of the imagination. Now, there should be like restrictions and

extensions in metaphysics as physics. We must settle
what are first and fundamental truths by scientific investigation ; and then, above this solid ground, we may allow a covering to be spread, rich as the clouds of the
evening sky.

IX.

Agnosticism appears in a variety of forms. In particular, it takes a vulgar and a philosophic form. In the
former, it is obliged to admit the sensible, but turns away
from all the higher truths of God and immortality ; of
these, it is said, we can know nothing. It is obliged, in
spite of itself, practically to acknowledge reality in the
common affairs of life — at least in regard to meat and
money ; but would leave all spiritual truth in the regions
of doubt and darkness. In this shape it is an impression
and a vague credulity, rather than a fixed conviction and
faith ; and in arguing with it we feel as if we were fight-
ing with a ghost. It is only when attacked that it takes
the form of a fixed creed. Thus put it claims to a philosophy ; and puts itself in the form of a general doctrine. It is of vast moment in these circumstances to
have a decision in the final court of appeal, and to show
that agnosticism is utterly untenable, being contrary to
our fundamental cognitions. This is what I have endeavored to do in this treatise, leaving the vulgar agnosticism without a foundation.

X.

In closing this paper, I may remark that our spontaneous belief that we are in the midst of reality, gives us
a feeling of assurance and stability in all the affairs, in-

cluding the practical affairs, of life. It goes with us, and should be encouraged to go with us, wherever we go. It is the business of philosophy not to undermine and restrain it, but to explain and defend it.

Physicists, in their deeper researches, are ever coming to mysteries which they are apt to designate as metaphysics. What should they do in these circumstances? When there is a reasonable hope of going farther, they should just continue their researches on the method prescribed by the logic of science. But when they have come to a truly metaphysical truth, — when they have come to a first truth, to what is self-evident and necessary, to what shines in its own light, and rests on its own foundation, — then they should feel that they have come to the rock, and should rest and be satisfied. This they should always do when they come to what is self-evidently real. It should be one main end of metaphysical philosophy to furnish to them the tests of such truths, with an arrangement and classified list of them. This I have endeavored to do in my work on " First and Fundamental Truth." What is found deficient in that work will doubtless be supplied by others.

It is only on the supposition of things within and without us being real, that we have logical proof of the existence of God. " The invisible things of God are clearly seen, being understood from the things that are made, even his eternal power and Godhead." It is from *the things that are made* we get a legitimate argument for what we do not see, the existence of the Maker. As long as we look on what we perceive as mere phenomena, sensations, or subjective ideas, the God we reach must be of a like character, ideal or pantheistic.

Every student of the history of religion knows that philosophy and theology are apt to affect each other. A high theology has often elevated philosophy by bringing in its high ideas, so allied to religion and to God. A pretentious philosophy, passing beyond its proper sphere, has often corrupted religion. Even the grand systems of Plato and Aristotle have been made to corrupt the simplicity of the faith, as we may see in Origen, in the ancient Church, and in the scholastic writers of mediæval times, and in the pantheistic systems. The holy doctrines of the Church in Germany have had more influence than any other external power in constraining philosophy to look to the highest attributes of man, his freedom, his personality, and his immortality. A meagre theology, overlooking the higher perfections of God, has favored an empirical philosophy. The sensational philosophy has produced a theology which takes no account of the holiness of God. The rationalism of England, in the end of last century and the beginning of this, allied itself with the theory which accounted for all our ideas by association, and with utilitarianism. The ideal philosophy gives us an ideal theology, which tends toward pantheism, and has produced those plausible theories which have come over to us from Germany.

We claim to be formed in the image of God, and a realistic philosophy, teaching us to look to the various powers of man, should raise our faith to the contemplation of a full-orbed Deity: our understanding leading us to look on him as omniscient, our moral nature to regard him as holy and just, and our feelings to cleave to him as benevolent. The full truth revealed by theology and philosophy is: God is a Spirit; God is Light; God is Love.

APPENDIX.

———•———

APPENDIX A.

ARISTOTLE ON THE COGNITIVE POWER OF THE MIND.

EVER since Descartes, the Father of Modern Philosophy, drew so decidedly the distinction between mind and body, there has been a change of view among metaphysicians generally as to what the mind starts with in its intelligent acts, and as to the nature of sense-perception. Descartes, who was so resolute a defender of spiritualism, maintained that mind cannot act directly on body, nor body upon mind. To explain their evident intercourse, Malebranche, following Descartes, taught the doctrine of Occasional Causes; Locke called in Ideas; and Leibnitz advocated Preëstablished Harmony, to show how mind could know body. None of these theories could accomplish the end they were meant to serve; could in any way explicate the nature of perception by the senses. The Idea, as has been shown by Reid and Hamilton, only brought in new difficulties, only introduced officious intermeddlers. It may be profitable in these circumstances to turn to the views of Aristotle. These were commonly adopted by the schoolmen throughout the thousand years of mediæval times.

It is evident that he gives a higher, or rather a deeper, place to native cognition than is now done. In treating of the intellectual powers, the moderns speak of the Senses and of the discursive faculties of Judgment and of Reasoning, which is made up of correlated judgments. But they neglect to announce that the senses, external and internal, give knowledge of realities; and judgments imply real or imaginary objects, on which they are pronounced. Our judgments are always predications about something apprehended. They are the declaration of a relation between two or more things which, in the order of things and of time, must be prior to the judgments upon them. To judge or reason, we must have objects about which to judge or reason. The unit of thought is not, as Hamilton and most modern metaphysicians maintain, judgment, but cognition by sense-perception and self-consciousness. What we start with in intelligence is knowledge, and thus and then the judgment has materials on which to act, and may rise to higher cognitions of realities by observing further relations between things, and drawing conclusions.

The judgments may be about objects, imaginary as well as real. But imaginations are formed of things which we have experienced, put in new forms and dispositions. Our judgments about them do not make them real, but they imply a reality, from which the imaginations have been drawn. Our idea of a mermaid is derived from the woman and the fish. Our systems of Psychology will ever be perplexed and confused till they give knowledge of concrete things a primary place in the operations of the mind, and make judgment depend upon it.

Aristotle's Divisions of the Powers of the Soul. — I do not claim that the Stagyrite has stated all that I have now laid down, but he has given a higher or rather a deeper place to cognition than the moderns.

His penetration allured him to draw innumerable distinctions among the powers of the soul. It might be argued, I think, that all these proceed on real differences. But I have not been able to discover that he sums them up in a comprehensive unity. He does not profess to give an exhaustive and logical classification of the mental powers. The parts are not exclusive and independent.

Perhaps his most fundamental division of the faculties is that noticed by Sir W. Hamilton into the Gnostic and Orective, adopted by Aristotle's commentator, Philoponus.

This is a distinction, noticed not only by Philoponus, but by others who follow Aristotle, such as Thomas Aquinas, who, in philosophy, seems to me to be the most judicious of the schoolmen. (See Appendix B.)

In *De Anima*, II. 2, Nutritive, Sense-Perception, Discursive, Motive, θρεπτικόν, αἰσθητικόν, διανοητικόν, κίνησις.

Again, *De Anima*, II. 3, Nutrition, Sense-Perception, Appetence, Local Motive, Discursive Power, θρεπτικόν, αἰσθητικόν, ὀρεκτικόν, κινητικὸν κατὰ τόπον, διανοητικόν.

Again, *De Anima*, III. 10, Nutrition, Sense-Perception, Cognition, Will, Appetence, θρεπτικόν, αἰσθητικόν, νοητικόν, βουλευτικόν, ὀρεκτικόν.

Throwing out nutrition, which is a physiological process, and taking sense-perception and the discursive power together, as cognitive powers, and similarly together Will and Appetence, we have the two forms, the Cognitive and Motive.

He sums up the powers in two groups, under a different nomenclature : —

De Anima, III. 9, τὸ κριτικόν and τὸ κινεῖν τὴν κατὰ τόπον κίνησιν (τὸ κινητικόν) ; discerning and motive.

De Anima, III. 9, If a tripartite division of the soul is made, in each there is ὄρεξις, for Will is in the rational or intelligent part ; and in the non-rational part, desire and impulse, ἡ ἐπιθυμία καὶ ὁ θυμός.

So we have the Soul defined as that in which we live, perceive, and think, that is, the Vital principle, Sense-Perception, and Discursive Power, II. 2.

"The part of the Soul which is rational is divisible into two: the Will (βουλευτικόν), and the Intelligent (ἐπιστημονικόν). That these are different from one another, may appear from their objects (ὑποκείμενα). For as color and flavor and sound and odor are different from one another, so nature has made the perception of them different : sound we have through the hearing sense, flavor by the taste, and color by the sight ; so, likewise, we must assume the same arrangement elsewhere, namely, that, since the objects differ, there are different parts of the soul by which we get knowledge of them. That which is perceived by the reason (τὸ νοητόν) is different from that which is perceived by the senses; and as we know both by the mind, there must therefore be a part which has to do with the objects of sense-perception, different from that which has to do with the things perceived by the reason." This last quotation is from the "Magna Moralia" (I. 35), which, if not written by Aristotle, was written by some one who felt his influence.

Aristotle on Sense-Perception. — There is the frequently quoted passage : " Sense-Perception is the power of perceiving the form (εἶδος) of sensible objects without the accompanying matter (ὕλη), just as the wax takes the figure of the seal without the iron or gold which makes the ring." *De Anima*, II. 12.

He enunciates what I regard as the true doctrine, and which I have quoted in the text. *De Sensu*, 2, τὸ αἰσθητὸν ἐνεργεῖν ποιεῖ τὴν αἴσθησιν.

He gives to the senses the power of a certain kind of knowledge. "Animals participate in a certain kind of knowledge, some more, some less, some, indeed, very little ; they have sense-perception, and sense-perception is a certain kind of knowledge " : γνώσεώς τινος πάντα μετέχουσι, τὰ μὲν πλείονος, τὰ δ᾽ ἐλάττονος, τὰ δὲ πάμπαν μικρᾶς· αἴσθησιν γὰρ ἔχουσιν, ἡ δ᾽ αἴσθησις γνῶσίς τις. This passage is very decisive as to man, and all animals having knowledge, — a certain kind of knowledge. *De Anim. Gen.*, I. 23.

He assures us that the perceptions of the senses are always true, αἱ μὲν αἰσθήσεις ἀληθεῖς αἰεί. *De Anima*, III. 3.

He shows that the deceptions of the senses are merely apparent. He saw that the difficulties might be cleared up by attending to what each sense testifies, and separating the associated imagination and opinions, or judgments. *De Anima*, III. 1, 3, 6.

He tells us : " It is not possible to have knowledge till one comes to individual things." *Metaph.*, I. 2, 11.

He announces a realistic doctrine : " A man can think (νοῆσαι) whenever he wishes, but not so exercise perception, for the object must be there :" διανοῆσαι μὲν ἐπ᾽ αὐτῷ, ὁπόταν βούληται, αἰσθάνεσθαι δ᾽ οὐκ ἐπ᾽ αὐτῷ : ἀναγκαῖον γὰρ ὑπάρχειν τὸ αἰσθητόν. *De Anima*, II. 5.

" The sensible object removed removes the perception, but the perceptive faculty, on the other hand (removed), does not remove the object of perception ": τὸ μὲν αἰσθητὸν ἀναιρεθὲν συναναιρεῖ τὴν αἴσθησιν, ἡ δ' αἴσθησις τὸ αἰσθητὸν οὐ συναιρεῖ. *Categor.*, 5.

Aristotle has not only individual senses, he has a master sense, τὸ κύριον αἰσθητήριον, or a common sense, κοινὴ αἴσθησις. This faculty distinguishes between the different sorts of Sense-Perception, sight, taste, etc., and synthesizes and comprehends various perceptions as belonging to one object, *De Anima*, III. " There is a common power which accompanies all the separate parts, by which the mind perceives alike that it sees and that it hears ; for not by the sense of sight does the mind see that it sees ; and it distinguishes, and is able to distinguish, for example, that 'sweet' is different from 'bright,' neither by taste nor by sight, nor by both these together, but by some common faculty ('mental part,' μόριον), working with all the instruments of sense-perception. For perception is single, and the master sense is single." *De Somno*, II.

It is to be regretted, I think, that at the time of Aristotle, and for some ages after, the Greeks had not given a place to self-consciousness. To it should have been allotted the power which the mind has of seeing that it sees. I believe it was not till towards the time of M. Aurelius, in the middle of the second century after Christ, that self-consciousness, συνείδησις, had a separate and important place allotted to it.

Metaphysicians will find it necessary in these times, when philosophical inquiry seems to be tending towards nescience, to look to and consider the views held by the great leader of thought for a millennium, and by those who were led by him. Reality, with the capacity of knowing it, is the one thing necessary to make knowledge consistent in itself, and consistent with our nature. It is the one thing needful to introduce in order to meet the agnosticism to which Huxley and Spencer are reducing all philosophical inquiry. The common opponents of Spencer and of agnosticism leave this out, and their replies are inconclusive, and are felt to be unsatisfactory.

APPENDIX B.

It may serve a good purpose to give the views of Saint Thomas, the angelical doctor, on the same subjects (" Summa Theologica," P. 1, *Quaest.* lxxxv. 6). He quotes Augustine: Omnis qui fallitur, id in quo fallitur, non intelligit. Aristotle is quoted as " the Philosopher " : intellectus semper est verus. He discusses his subject, and his conclusion is : Cum quidditas rei sit proprium objectum intellectus, nunquam contingit circa ipsum falli nisi per accidens, prout ipsi compositio vel divisio, seu discursus admiscetur, in quibus fallitur quandoque. He approves Aristotle : Sensus enim circa proprium objectum non decipitur, sicut visus circa colorem, nisi forte per accidens in impedimento circa organum contingente. He sums up : Ad *primum* ergo dicendum quod falsitas dicitur esse in mente secundum compositionem et divisionem. Et similiter dicendum est ad *secundum* de opinione et ratiocinatione. Et ad *tertium* de errore peccantium qui consistit in applicatione ad appetibile. Sed in absoluta consideratione quidditatis rei et eorum quae per eam cognoscuntur, intellectus nunquam decipitur.

APPENDIX C.

RECENT CRITICISMS OF KANT.

There are some indications that the recoil against the combined Idealism and Nescience of Kant has commenced. Dr. Hutchison Stirling announces emphatically that Kant has not answered Hume, and that never has the world been so befooled by a system as it has been befooled by the system of Kant. He uses very strong language. He declares the system of Kant to be " a vast and prodigious failure," and his method as only " a laborious, baseless, inapplicable superfetation." — *Princeton Review*, Jan., 1879.

I may quote a little more fully from Stählen : " Kant's aim was to vindicate the objectivity of human knowledge in opposition to the scepticism of Hume. This he deemed possible only in one way, namely, by showing that that which gives objective validity and necessity to our knowledge of things is to be found, not in the things themselves, but in the human mind itself." He goes on: "Kant's intention was to establish the reality of our knowledge in opposition to the scepticism of Hume. But what he meant to be a rescue turns out to be rather an entire overthrow of the knowledge of objective truth. For the method which he follows tends to show that what we know is merely the phenomenal appearance, not the truth nor the thing itself." But what is the phenomenal? The answer is, "Phenomenon in the Kantian sense *is not objective but subjective* phenomenon, that is, it is not a coming to light or coming forward of the thing itself, but purely a mode in which we represent things, an affection of our sensibility, a modification of our consciousness which reveals nothing whatever of the nature of the thing as it is in itself."

This, I may remark, is the very objection which I have been taking for years past, that Kant makes the mind start with appearances instead of things, and that we cannot know things except under forms imposed by our own minds. He insists: "Objective knowledge, a knowledge of anything that has actuality outside and independently of our consciousness, there is none." This is true not only of things external to ourselves, but of the mind itself, as Kant is constantly asserting that "we do not know even ourselves, but merely as we appear to ourselves." He says I have no right to say that a thing is, if I am in entire ignorance how or what it is (p. 26), an objection which, I may add, I have been constantly taking. I have been particularly pleased with the following extract from Zeller: — "But, however unworthy of acknowledgment the prudence with which Kant refrained from drawing the extreme conclusions of his idealism, it must not be forgotten that this very course involved him in great difficulties. Not only when the general postulates of his system were denied, but also when these were admitted, there were still to be found many profoundly critical questions left unanswered, many a doubt unsolved. This was true especially of Kant's positions concerning

the thing in itself (*Ding an Sich*). On the one hand, for instance, on the supposition that direct experience presents things
to us only under the forms of perception and thought, only as
phenomena, the question could still be raised whether it had
really been proven that the essence of things is of necessity unknowable for us, whether we possess no means of determining
their essence through the observation and comparison of phenomena. If, on the other hand, the complete incognizability of
the thing in itself was granted, the question still emerged, whence,
then, can we obtain any knowledge of its bare existence? If I
know absolutely nothing of *what* an object is, I cannot know
whether it is, and *that* it is; for every assertion concerning the
existence of a thing presupposes some concept of the thing whose
existence is affirmed, no matter how incomplete this concept
may be. When Kant endeavored to show the existence of things
outside us, he understood by these at best some reality apart
from us, which occasions our sensations; when he demanded
belief in a Deity, he understood by Deity the independent cause
of the world. When, on the other hand, he maintained that we
can know absolutely nothing of the thing in itself, that it is an
unknown X, a mere problematic or limitative concept, this re-
quired that he should leave it completely undetermined whether
any reality apart from us exists at all. His explanation of the
idea of cause as a category of the understanding, which as such
is applicable to phenomena alone, should have prevented him
from applying it to the thing in itself, from postulating this thing
as the cause of our presentations. Nay, he should have gone
further, and have said straight out that we have no ground for
the assumption of the thing in itself, that it is of no service in
the explanation of phenomena, that it only marks the limit of
our activity, and as such it can in itself lie just as well within as
without us. This deduction was in reality drawn before long in
the Kantian school, the more readily, the more undeniable it is
that Kant's refutation of idealism, and his moral argument for
the existence of God, are far removed from the validity of strict
demonstration." — Zeller's " Geschichte der deutschen Philoso-
phie seit Leibnitz," pp. 414, 415 (second edition).

APPENDIX D.

THE OFFICE OF INDUCTION IN FUNDAMENTAL PHILOSOPHY.

I have had great difficulty in getting a hearing for one point in my philosophic views. In the discovery of *a priori* truth I allot an important function to inductive observation. This seems to identify me with the empiricists, from whom I entirely separate myself. I hold that there is no induction in the spontaneous exercise of intuition; it sees the object at once. But if we, as metaphysicians, express the law in a general form or law, we need to proceed by a careful observation, the facts being given us by self-consciousness. We have to inquire what is the precise *a priori* law, say of causation, as it manifests itself. If we neglect to do this, there is a great risk of presenting the principle in a mutilated, which is, so far, an erroneous form. The vagaries of metaphysicians commonly spring from an imperfect induction. But in calling in induction we do not give it an authoritative or guaranteeing office. Induction merely lets us know what the law in the mind is; it does not give it its imperativeness. It needs anxious inspection to find what the law of causation is, but the law operates whether we observe it or not. This distinction is easily understood by those disposed to give their attention. It saves me from the inconsistency and the imbecility with which I have been charged in a recent criticism. It gives to reason and to observation each its proper place in the construction of fundamental philosophy. It may be made the means of reconciling the Scottish and German philosophies.